ROOT ACCESS LIFE

JOAH RALF

Copyright © 2024 Joah Ralf

The moral right of the author has been asserted.

Apart from any fair dealing for the purposes of research or private study, or criticism or review, as permitted under the Copyright, Designs and Patents Act 1988, this publication may only be reproduced, stored or transmitted, in any form or by any means, with the prior permission in writing of the publishers, or in the case of reprographic reproduction in accordance with the terms of licences issued by the Copyright Licensing Agency. Enquiries concerning reproduction outside those terms should be sent to the publishers.

Troubador Publishing Ltd
Unit E2 Airfield Business Park
Harrison Road, Market Harborough
Leicestershire LE16 7UL
Tel: 0116 279 2299
Email: books@troubador.co.uk
Web: www.troubador.co.uk

ISBN 978 1 80514 511 0

British Library Cataloguing in Publication Data.
A catalogue record for this book is available from the British Library.

Printed and bound in Great Britain by 4edge Limited
Typeset in 12pt Minion Pro by Troubador Publishing Ltd, Leicester, UK

INTRODUCTION

You are not a pawn that can only move in one direction. What you are, is a queen.

If you have never played chess before, let me tell you that all chess pieces have limited ability to move. The pawn can only move in one direction, one step at a time, and it can only capture other chess pieces one step diagonally. The knight, the bishop, the rook can only do one specific move and the king can only walk one step to each side. The queen, on the other hand, can move in every direction, freely back and forth, as far as she wants. She can effortlessly move to every field of the chessboard, while other chess pieces are limited. If the queen moves horizontally from one side of the chessboard to the other, she can simply move back diagonally to the opposite side. The queen can see the chessboard from every angle and completely change her point of view with every move. Let me tell you, on the chessboard of life, you are a queen! In fact, all of us can be a queen. We can change the angle in which we see the world. We are limitless in the directions we can go or the points of view we can take. Furthermore, after we have been to see one angle of the world, we can continue moving. Straight to another point, or perhaps even back to where we were before. On the chessboard of life, we do not have to choose one square field to remain on forever. Without having to completely change our mind or ourselves, we can move our perceptions and go and see all angles. We can learn from every standpoint we are in and we are always free to go back, or to a totally new place.

Do not limit yourself to only one possible move or to look and go in only one direction. On the chessboard of life, you are not a pawn that can never move backwards. You are not a knight that can only jump on certain fields, or a bishop that can only move either on the black or on the white squares. You are not a rook that can never move diagonally or a king that can only do one step at a time. You are a queen. We are all as versatile and capable as a queen, we just have to realize that and make use of it.

As we have by far the most complex brain of any species in the world, we humans are the most versatile, most capable, but also the most complicated living beings. While it is an extremely useful and powerful machine that we carry around day by day, the complexity of our brain can be overwhelming. Using the immense power of our brain in ensemble with our body and our emotions constructively is not easy. Social norms, natural instincts, perfectionism, limiting beliefs, thoughts of doubt, fear, imagined problems, cravings, obsessions and egoism dictate us.

> *It is a man's own mind, not his enemy or foe, that lures him to evil ways.*
> – Buddha

Some of our desires, behaviors and reactions may be consciously driven. Others seem to be imprinted into our genes and implanted into our brains and bodies' core system. While we have all the power to use our brain in a self-determined way, endless programs and settings run our brain subconsciously. Endless habits and doctrines dictate our beliefs. They dictate which fields on the chessboard we are able to go to and how freely we are able to move. Yet, beneath our programming, we are free to choose which fields to visit and what moves to make. This book provides the perspectives and the thought-provoking material to move our viewpoints and thoughts more freely on the chessboard of life.

> *Were I to await perfection, my book would never be finished.*
> – Tai T'ung

ROOT ACCESS LIFE

It was smartphones that inspired me to come up with the concept of *Root Access Life*. Smartphones come with multiple factory settings that we can control and tweak. Yet they also come with programs and settings over which we have no influence. The manufacturer of a phone or an operating system has coded these functions into the core system. For a general user, it seems impossible to understand all programs or to alter all possible settings and there is often little interest in doing so. After all, smartphones work just fine as they are, right? Well, they work fine; they are just not fully understood and controlled by us as the user. Many programs and processes run in the background of our smartphone without our knowing. And some settings and functions are invisible to us or impossible for us to change.

This has brought me to a realization about our brain. It acts similarly to an operating system of an electronic device like a smartphone. Figuratively speaking, all of us have programs installed on our core system, inside our brain. These are tribal instincts and genetically programmed drives, as well as socially installed settings.

Most of us own a smartphone and we are fine using it as it is, with pre-installed settings and programs. Similarly, many of us do not bother to change or influence the default settings in our own operating system. We tend to follow general belief systems and typical behavioral patterns with little awareness, just as we are unaware of all the processes and programs that are active in the background of our phone. Unfortunately, plenty of our humanly behavioral patterns, habits and beliefs are not always conducive. Wouldn't it be great if we could understand the programming in our mind and perhaps even make changes to some of our settings?

On many electronic devices, like smartphones and computers, it is possible to do a kind of "hack" and get administrator-level access to the system. This is called "root access". "Root access" gives us privileged permissions on a computer system. It is the highest access, which enables us to perform functions that general users are not authorized to perform.

While I am not an expert of computers, nor of "root access", looking into this topic made one thing clear to me: there has to be a way to, figuratively speaking, gain "root access" in our brain and to get administrator-level access to our own life. Like a smartphone or a computer, we have a software with programs and settings. So, it has to be possible to understand these programs and alter our settings. To gain authority over our brains' operating systems and perform privileged functions, we need what I call "Root Access Life". It is the "root access" we can get not on a technical device but in our own mind and in our own life.

On our smartphones, we know how to use the apps and how to operate the general functions. But we do not understand most of the programming on our phone and exactly what it does in the background. On a smartphone or a computer, the knobs in the settings are sometimes grayed out or not visible to us at all. So we cannot operate these settings. That is also how we can think of Root Access Life. Many of our settings are grayed out or invisible to us at this moment. But they can become visible and they may be possible to alter. Root Access Life is the technical root access we apply to our human operating system, to our thinking and to the way we live. Some people might have more settings grayed out than others and some people are more willing to see their settings than others. Whatever the case may be, using Root Access Life does not ensure ideal settings. It simply refers to the ability to access and understand our programs and settings in the first place. From there, we are much more autonomous and can take more ownership and responsibility over ourselves, our thoughts and actions.

How Do We Get Root Access Life?

In order to gain root access on a phone, we have to first know that it exists and be willing to activate it. Then we have to be willing to learn about the operating system and its programming, because root access on a phone doesn't do much if we don't have any desire to understand or modify the system, or if we don't know what to do with it. The same is true for Root Access Life. Just as most people don't desire to understand the settings and background processes on their phone, many may not desire to know about the programs inside their own brain. Manufacturers don't offer phones that have root access by default. Similarly, we may not see through our programming by default. While gaining Root Access Life does not ensure the best use of the system, it opens the door for greater understanding and consciousness.

If you are not eager to look into your

own operating system and recognize your programming, then you are bound to predetermined moves. But if you are determined to understand your operating system and apprehend its settings, in every new situation, you are free like a queen. So, the willingness to acknowledge our own programming and default settings is the first, most important step towards Root Access Life.

The second step for activating Root Access Life is to challenge our mind into thinking outside of the box and beneath our programming and settings. Which is what the following chapters of this book are intended to do.

"Why should I get control over background processes on my phone, it works just fine the way it comes out of the box, right?"

"Why would I want to understand how the phone's operating system works and not just let it do its job?"

The same questions could be applied to our mind and our life. Why would you want to understand or change your own settings or understand your own programming? It is convenient and easy not to question our programming and to simply live by the rules of a society and by our natural impulses. The convenient way is to adopt the popular life advice and to conform to the settings that the general society gives us. Or to follow our impulses and natural wants and needs mindlessly. This might give us less work, but it also makes us more externally and subconsciously controlled, with default settings similar to a smartphone or a computer. What if our settings and programming cause problems? What if we want to think bigger and achieve and create something extraordinary? What if we want to know the truth, without settling for biased or ordinary answers? In that case, we need to challenge our default settings and make an effort to understand them.

As a baby or a child, we are very vulnerable and we are very limited in our physical abilities and experiences. Naturally, we are dependent on our caretakers and other adults that surround us. We are dependent on learning from them and adopting their beliefs. Throughout our lives we have many teachers and we are taught many lessons that code our brain. While this can fill up our brain with useful information, it does not necessarily train our autonomous thinking, our inner wisdom and ingenuity.

> *Education is the kindling of a flame,*
> *not the filling of a vessel.*
> – Socrates

Only by thinking independently and by making our personal experience and conclusions can we truly grow wise. There are endless great teachers in this world, but if we do not think about, or actively try to use, the taught skills, all teachings are of little use. If our settings are set in stone and we are not willing to change them, we simply copy programs, but we do not grow and unfold our own system. We could play an instrument to the exact notes we are given, or we can create our own symphony. Root Access Life requires the confidence to think for ourselves and independently and the confidence to move freely like a queen. Using Root Access Life, we can get more clarity over our mind and the programs that run us. We can see how our basic settings are set up, what programming we have been given and what adjustments we are able to make. Just as with a phone or any electronic device, it is almost impossible to understand every single function of an operating system, as we are not the manufacturer ourselves. We can, however, try to understand it as much as possible and try to use it in a smart way.

The point of this book is not to give you strict rules or new settings and programming. The point of this book is to inspire you to activate root access to your own operating system.

You may already have Root Access Life activated and you may already move freely like a queen in many areas. In any case, Root Access Life can be activated or deactivated in different areas if we do not pay attention.

We activate it when we genuinely want to see our programming. We deactivate it when we don't want to see them. We activate it when we genuinely want to see the objective truth. We deactivate it when we just want to be right. We activate it when we move like a queen, to see all sides of the spectrum, and it is deactivated if we choose to only stand on one field.

Whether or not you agree with all the details in this book, the analogy of Root Access Life can bring anyone to think and to at least question their own settings and programming. If you can think about the ideas and concepts in this book autonomously and even put them into question, then you have understood what it means to make use of Root Access Life.

I would like to emphasize that I am writing this book on even ground. In my own life, I have been convinced of default and biased views that have later turned out to be faulty or inadequate. I had preconceptions that turned out to be invalid and I was driven by programs and settings I was oblivious to. I could now claim that through Root

Access Life I am free of programming and always unbiased. But, of course, that would be nonsense. I will step into such automated and programmed thinking again in the future. I will make more wrong assumptions and I will be misled by information. The fact that we can acknowledge this gives us the key. The will to see through our programming, as best we can, opens the door.

If you are excited to understand your programming, to question your default settings and challenge your way of thinking, you most certainly have the willingness to use Root Access Life. This is the first step. The second step is to learn about your programming and how to pierce past them.

That is how you get Root Access Life.

PROGRAMMING AND SETTINGS

Everybody should learn to program a computer, because it teaches you how to think.
– Steve Jobs

The programming and settings on our operating system must either stem from our genetics, which are given to us by birth, or from whatever we learn and experience after we are born. The society we grew up in, such as the society we live in at this moment, and our parents or caretakers have profound effects on how we see the world. On what we believe and even on what we desire, like or dislike. On the other hand, there are strong programs that we are given by nature, embedded into our genes. To illustrate this further, I divide our programming and settings into two categories:

- "Recognizable and unchangeable programming".
- "Recognizable and changeable setting".

Recognizable and Unchangeable Programming

The programming that we are given by nature and before birth is not simply to be changed.

But it is recognizable and partially understandable, as we can understand how it influences us and comprehend why we have it. Hunger and thirst, for example, are natural programs over which we have little influence. We can only understand how the need for food and drink affects our body and we can adjust our actions based on this understanding. These types of programs also include, for example, sexual needs, the desire to be liked and accepted, such as the desire to be happy and fulfilled, to expand and grow. As well as the programming of our unique character, individual qualities and much more. You see, genetically coded programs are obviously not generally a bad thing. The programs that we are given by birth are mostly necessary and their existence is evolutionarily explainable. In any case, we can't completely change them or shut them down, no matter how hard we try. But we can appreciate them. We can learn to understand how they affect us and how to make wise decisions in respect of them. Primarily, we can accept that these instinctual programs exist and that they have their purpose. We can learn to deal with impulses, wants and needs appropriately and channel them into a constructive direction. But in societies around the world, many natural instincts are demonized or even denied. The instinct of sexual desire is stigmatized, the want to be the best is called egoistic, the craving for unhealthy food is called undisciplined. But sexual desires, the desire to be special and successful or the cravings for calorically dense foods are all very natural instincts and they are genetically given to us. All natural instincts have their reasonings and there is no point in denying or stigmatizing them.

Another typical instinctual programming is wanting to be accepted or liked by others. Unless we are completely miserable, this natural program has an effect on all of us to a certain extent and it is given to us by birth. The reason one might say, "I don't care what others think," is perhaps to make others think that they are very cool and tough. They don't want others to think that they care what others are thinking. Which would again imply that they do care what other people think. This is an example of how we can deny our natural programs, pretending that they don't exist. But we can all admit to ourselves that we have a certain instinct that makes us want to be liked and accepted by others. We can accept that this program has its use and purpose and we can then live with it appropriately. Without letting it dictate our life. Simply acknowledging and accepting this natural program is a way of using Root Access Life. Because it is a way of looking into our operating system and understanding it.

If we observe human beings, including ourselves, it seems that we ignore many of our natural programs or are oblivious to them. While we are very influenced by our genetical impulses at times, we often react to them automatically and without awareness. Being unaware, our programs can run us, like background functions that run on our smartphone. When someone says something provocative, we tend to get provoked. Something unpleasant happens; we tend to react with bad temper. When we are angry, we tend to insult other people. Someone is rude to us; we tend to react back in a rude way. Anger, among many other emotions, is a natural program that we all have installed and that we are all capable of experiencing. There is nothing wrong with being angry at times. The problem arises when our anger is so deeply coded that it operates automatically and without our influence.

All too often we let our natural programming dictate us, and other people or situations can turn on and off like a switch. But we have it free will and an opportunity to choose where we put our focus and how we act every second of every day. Knowing about Root Access Life does not mean that we always make perfect decisions. But making use of Root Access Life means that we are aware of our natural, genetic programming as much as possible and that we will not deny it. From there on, we always have the free will to change our behaviors and our focus.

Recognizable and Changeable Settings

Whatever we program on our system after we are born is what O call "recognizable and changeable settings". While our natural, birth-given desires and instincts can't be completely changed or undone, socially determined settings can be acknowledged and even modified. Just as those natural, genetical programs, a lot of socially determined settings have their own important purpose. As we grow up, we learn to behave appropriately and to function properly in a society. This makes sense and is absolutely reasonable, as long as these social norms do not blind us to different perspectives. Happily dancing and singing at a funeral would not be appropriate in my culture. In other cultures, however, happily dancing and singing at a funeral is completely normal. We don't necessarily have to fight against such unwritten social laws, but we better not let them dictate our convictions. If we grew up in one society, we would perhaps have the setting that it is right to dance at a funeral. Growing up in another society, we learn to have a completely different stance. The way we act and the things we believe and prefer do not always have to be changed, but it makes sense to see them objectively. To see such socially determined settings as what they are. When we truly understand how we are influenced by social constructs, it gives us the opportunity to "reset" ourselves or to change specific settings. It is through awareness and through changing our point of view that we can truly choose our own beliefs and actions freely. If we are too close-minded to look at other cultures, we will never know that there are other ways to perform funerals. If we are not aware of the social settings that run us, we will never question them. But as soon as we are willing to see them and understand them, they have no power over us. So then they can be changed and we can refocus, if we wish to do so. Because taking different points of view, dissenting from our current programming, we automatically launch Root Access Life, as it is a way of outsmarting our settings and programming, to see beneath them.

Sometimes we can change a socially wired setting. Sometimes it's enough to simply acknowledge it. It is hindering, however, if we deny it, or are barred against becoming aware of it in the first place. Because that leaves us externally controlled and unable to make changes in our very own operating system when necessary.

We are all, in part, socially programmed in how we talk and behave, what we do, like, believe and in what we believe to be good or bad, right or wrong. So the question is not whether or not we are programmed, but whether or not we are capable of investigating and partially influencing our programming and settings.

Many doctrines in our society are only useful to a degree. For example, "money only comes through hard work", "if you want anything in life, you need to put in a lot of effort" or "good things aren't free". While such ideas hold some truth, they can also hinder us if we never reassess them. Perhaps we don't feel good enough or deserving if we do not constantly work hard. Or perhaps we do not value things if they are available and easily accessible. If we watch a free video that teaches us three steps to improve an area of our life, we probably don't implement the steps seriously, because they were taught for free. If, however, we pay a large sum of money to participate in a course that teaches us the exact same steps, we pay very close attention and make sure to implement them carefully. Our invested time and money make us focus more and we perceive the same thing as more valuable as their price goes up. We may have been taught that more money and material things will make us happy. So we discard the simple and beautiful moments that could give us much more joy and a fulfilled life. Questioning societal doctrines and outsmarting our own biases is what leads us past our programming and into the roots of our central operating system.

The most dangerous programs and settings are those that are rooted so deeply that they trigger an automated reaction in us. The ones that we obey with blindness and a complete lack of awareness. The human mind is fascinating and incredibly useful. But deliberately underestimating its flaws is one of those flaws itself. Our brain is smart, but be humble enough to see its limits, its automated, lazy and programmed responses. It is not my suggestion and it is not realistic to constantly be aware of all our programs and settings. Yet it is possible to see them when the situation requires it, or when we get confronted with new information.

Natural human emotions and desires can be very similar from person to person but the way we react to them and the way we process them can be very different. We all feel the need to be accepted and liked by others, to grow and unfold ourselves, the need for love and affection, pleasure and dopamine. We all have feelings of doubt sometimes, feelings of insecurity, of anger, grief or anxiety. Sometimes we might feel in the wrong place, weak and inferior. Sometimes we might feel boisterous, energetic or even aggressive, egoistic and evil. To respond wisely, we have to understand that we are not slaves to doctrines, our emotions, thoughts or wants and needs, which I refer to as settings and programming. They are a part of us and they have a big impact, but our own choices influence the direction of our life. We can choose to react like a coded machine or we can choose to act and react freely like a queen.

> *Root Access Life is what you apply when you look beneath your programming into your mind and soul. In the exact moment when you challenge your own programming and belief systems, you have Root Access Life.*

FOLLOWING THE MAJORITY

On the chessboard of life, a queen does not blindly follow other chess pieces, she goes wherever she wants to go and sees whatever angle she wants to see. This chapter is meant to illustrate the way our programs let us be steered by the crowd surrounding us. The programming of mass dynamic is one that hinders us profoundly from being a queen, from using our entire abilities and from being free in thought and action. It wants us to be a pawn, going the same way as the others. Moving only in one direction, not looking back or to the sides and not seeing different points of view.
Root Access Life requires that we thoroughly understand the influence that the mass dynamic has on us.

Mass Dynamic

Most people are other people. Their thoughts are someone else's opinions, their lives a mimicry, their passions a quotation.
– Oscar Wilde

Shame is a natural feeling that prevents us from falling out of the line. We are naturally reluctant to feel shame and to catching too much negative attention from other people. How would it feel, for example, to be walking down a busy shopping street, loudly clapping, out of no reason, all by yourself? For most people, doing something like this is unthinkable. Yet it is absolutely harmless. Nothing life-threatening would happen. But our tribal instincts make us afraid of doing something weird or unaccepted and they make us feel ashamed. This aversion against feeling ashamed, such as many other human emotions, may be explained through our evolution. Living thousands of years ago, being despised by our tribe could be disastrous for us. Out alone in the wild, without companionship, would likely mean death. So we instinctively do not want to be excluded; we want to be accepted and we want to be part of the group. It is a natural, instinctual and deeply wired programming in our system that can be explained through evolution, as we have always wanted to ensure our well-being and survival.

It is fascinating how driven we are by the desire to be liked, accepted and to fit in. Even less social people and so-called introverts desire a feeling of being accepted in one way or another. The fear of being excluded is so deeply, genetically wired in us that we constantly tend to adjust our behaviors and our world views to that of the group. No matter how tough or cool we appear on the surface, deep inside we all want to feel approved, loved and accepted and we are afraid of being excluded from our group.

For most people, the preferred group to follow is logically the one with the largest sum of people and the mainstream of the society they live in. Some identify with a smaller mass of people and others form gangs of smaller numbers. All the same, it is the programming of wanting to fit into a group. So the same concept applies to smaller groups outside of the big crowd or the mainstream. It is, however, particularly influential in the large mass of a society. This aspiration of belonging somewhere and being accepted can be a positive thing, but it can also lead to irrational behavior if we do not see through it. There is no need to stop joining groups or to suppress the desire to be accepted by others. We should, however, be aware of the influence this desire has on our own convictions and actions. At least, if we want to move as freely as a queen.

In a world where billions of people live closely together, the pressure to fit in can be partially helpful. We treat each other with basic respect, we try to adapt to our social environment and we try to act appropriately, according to specific social norms. If there is a harmony in the group, there is support, there is cohesion and growth. But at the same time, the pressures of the masses can create one the most dangerous dynamics. The fear of being despised by society or the mass can lead masses of people to do what goes against every single person's individual values. This genetic program makes us desperate for being approved by others and sticking to the stream and the common rules. But if we do not question the standards of the group and scrutinize social norms ourselves, we are not acting on free will, but based on how we are genetically coded. We are not functioning autonomously but automatically. In today's world, it is not deadly not to fit in or not to be liked by everyone in a group. But our natural fears and instincts do not see a difference between now and hundreds of thousands of years ago and they still command us.

When a kid falls and slightly hurts its knee, it stands up and keeps running around, as if nothing has happened. Especially if nobody else is around. But if the kid's caretakers hysterically ask if everything is all right, it probably starts crying. Did we change since being that little kid? If the people in our surrounding get hysterical about something, are we hysterical too? If the people around us do not react to a certain information, will we ignore it too? How far are we steered by the people surrounding us and how much do we choose our own beliefs and actions? Social conformity experiments show that we tend to automatically follow what the group around us does or thinks, even if there is no logical reason for it. So when a belief becomes mainstream and adopted by the mass, more people will then be sucked into the mass dynamic. They assume that the belief must be right, as so many believe it. And the more people assume it must be right, the more then again assume it must be right. Without knowing much about the topic at hand, a large sum of people can figuratively crowd up and walk in one direction. This may be because of our tribal instincts, but also because we do not dare to imagine how something could be false, which so many people believe. Until we understand how our natural programming can create a mass dynamic. As protective and comprehendible as this programming may be, it can create a mass conviction similar to a mass panic. If, in a crowd, everyone panics, you panic too. Why would everyone panic if there wasn't anything to panic about, right? If, in a crowd, everyone believes something, you believe it too. Why would everyone believe it if it wasn't true, right? A mass panic could arise, because there is an actual threat. It could, however, also arise just by the panic itself and not because there is anything to panic about. This has been seen in large festivals, for example, where such tragedies have occurred. The same can be true in a mass belief. A mass belief could arise just through the mass dynamic itself, and not necessarily because it is most factual.

Don't confuse the truth with the opinion of the majority. – Jean Cocteau

"If most people do it, it must be right."

"If something actually worked, everyone would do it."

"If most people believe this, it must be perfectly proven, otherwise no one would believe it."

"Nobody would do it if it was wrong."

These are all similar codes in our system and different ways of saying, "I am going to do and believe what everyone does and believes, and simply not question it."

We tend to give our trust easily to whatever is the direction of most people and not necessarily to what makes most sense or is very evident. While it may initially make sense to follow the crowd, I would like you to rethink such programming. The biggest, the most trained, the most educated and the smartest fall into the trap of thinking that the mass must, in any case, be right. But there are good reasons why this rule does not always apply.

Few people are capable of expressing with equanimity opinions which differ from the prejudices of their social environment. Most people are even incapable of forming such opinions. – Albert Einstein

Imagine ten people of similar education and status sitting at a table, when suddenly a controversial topic arises. Then everyone starts voicing their opinion about the topic and the discussion gets more heated. If nine people support one side in the argument, that one person who supports another side will likely not be taken seriously by the others. Arguments against that single person will likely be accepted by the group, no matter how little sense they make. The acceptance towards that one person is very low. If it's eight against two at the table, the whole group will likely start making fun of the two and their views. If it is seven against three, it might get more intense and the larger group will try to come up with somewhat more logical arguments against the three. If the numbers are more equal, the separation of the groups and the hate against each other will presumably increase.

Of course, sitting at a table of ten people, there could be more sanity, depending on the individual people and whether or not they are willing to activate Root Access Life in a discussion. More wise individuals would take things less personally and try to objectively examine the subject matter. But let's say, instead of ten people, it was a hall of hundreds or thousands of people forming an opinion about a topic. Very soon, a clear dynamic starts to take place, where logical arguments tend to count less than the sum of people that support a claim. This is especially true as long as everyone has a similar authority ranking. As soon as authority figures step into the game, the same dynamic starts all over. Nine authority figures say one thing and one says something else and those nine will likely win more followers, and so forth. We could also apply this principle to the number of news stations, of politicians or official organizations that present a certain narrative.

When does logic and the truth actually win and not just the quantity of supporters? It is bold to say, and perhaps oversimplified, but, generally, we tend to stand on the side where most people stand and we look into the direction where most people look. Not necessarily because it makes most sense, but because of who and how many do it. But shouldn't it be more important what the actual arguments are? When everyone is looking this way, remember to also take a look that way. Because the whole spectrum always provides a totally different picture than looking in just one direction.

Being outnumbered, it may seem frustrating to contest the group. But it gets worse. Because, when you are willing to see a wider spectrum of view, there are countless unpleasant ways in which the majority tries to push you back in line. If the majority of a society did something wrong, has predicted something falsely or did something stupid, they can easily claim a silly reason or make a simple excuse to make it seem acceptable. Most will accept the excuse, because they are in the same boat. Additionally, one quickly gets classified as an evil human being, trying to challenge the ideological and politically correct views of a group. It is the easiest way a group discredits you while upholding their convictions and group dynamic.

Simply by claiming that you are a bad person and by giving you an unpleasant name.

Or anything is simply turned around and against you. If you point out something irrational that the group is doing, they will just turn it around and call you irrational. Because you are outnumbered, there is then little to do against such accusations. If you want to uncover a person's misconceptions, it's going to be very hard when the mass is on that person's side. But if you want to make someone look like a "bad" person and the majority wants the same, you are going to have an easy time. If everyone on the planet is a smoker, it is very easy to make smoking look healthy and hard to convince people that it is not. Whatever society wants to hear is easy to say, but what they don't want to hear is hard to say. If everybody on the planet is a smoker, the burden of truth should not be placed on those who claim that smoking is unhealthy. It should logically be placed on those who claim it is healthy. But nonsensically, in society, the burden of proof is most often placed, by default, on the outnumbered.

If you always agree with the majority, you get little confrontation, you easily get approval and you rarely have to argue or defend yourself. The group you are in will be on your side and will cheer you up. It's simple and rewarding. Perhaps there are many mainstream views that you agree with. I definitely do. But what happens when you, just for once, disagree with one them? If you have looked deeper into a specific topic, realizing that the views of the majority are too shallow or narrow. Perhaps, recognizing that the mass is not seeing the whole story or the big picture. How well is your opinion tolerated then? All of a sudden, your ideas have little room for discussion and your opinions and personality can quickly be shut down and significantly attacked.

Unfortunately, this is how we are coded to become social opportunists. Whatever makes us fit in, we tend to support and whatever makes us get despised, we tend to refuse. The critical part is that this is often not conscious, but automated opportunism. If you see through your programming, you could be an opportunist, consciously knowing that you are adjusting your stance. Perhaps to prove a point, consciously intended to fit in, to reach a goal or even with the bad intention to manipulate. At least you are aware of it. However, when programs run in our background, we become oblivious to our opportunistic behavior. We adjust our belief systems, not based on free will, but based on our programming, while being convinced it was our free will.

When we subconsciously let our programs run us, we can get overly convinced while our arguments, beliefs and moral values are constantly adjusted to that of the group. Would we see things exactly the same way if the group we associate with, the party we vote for or the ideological movement we follow, had a different view? Picture asking children in a group difficult questions. Sometimes, we can observe that when we ask one child in a group directly, it will first look at its friends, trying to figure out their answers. If the child was asked alone, without knowing the answers of the others, it would have answered more genuinely. This is a behavior we can observe just as much in adults, it is just a little less visually perceptible. Autonomic thinking is often overruled by the programming of mass dynamic if we are unaware. It takes courage and perhaps the knowledge of Root Access Life not to obey the mass by default, but to question it by default.

At this point, you might ask yourself if the mass dynamic is simply correlation. Meaning that people tend to believe what everyone believes because it makes most sense and not because of their instinct to follow the group. But if you think that the mainstream belief is always the one that makes most sense, I challenge you to look back in history. Examine if you agree with what most people supported or with the mainstream narrative of the past. Read the mainstream news decades or centuries ago. Very likely, you disagree with a lot of it. Or perhaps you agree with some of it, but certainly not with all of it. And that is exactly the point. Many times the mass might be right, but what if they are not in just one point? That one point could become fatal, because it remains undisputed. It is safe to assume that there are at least some areas where the mass was misled or does not see things quite right. This is because the majority does not always choose a narrative for its cleverness. Mainstream narratives are often chosen because they fit perfectly to our human instincts and programming. Because they fit perfectly with the desire to feel morally superior, to be lazy and not having to think much. Or because they provide a simple-sounding solution for our fears and sufferings. The current mass belief of the society you live in is probably based on a complex interplay of historical events, the programming of the people and the mainstream news and propaganda. In any case, what the majority believes is certainly not always exclusively based on the best available evidence or the most objective, rational, pragmatic and unbiased view.

While propaganda can be done in all directions and in all areas, it is the mainstream propaganda of a country that heavily influences the mainstream opinion and therefore the mass. When a new controversial topic arises, the vast majority of people tend to side with the mainstream news. This is the most convenient and it takes the least individual due diligence. It is also the easiest way to fit in a society right away and to quickly feel accepted and morally superior. Once propaganda has set the minds of the masses, anyone with a different opinion will be discredited or even defamed. It takes little effort to build our reality of life around the mainstream news and mainstream propaganda, but it is a limited reality, it is distorted and it is easily manipulated. Once an opinion is formed and the crowd is set to uniformly move in one direction, it seems like an impossible mission to contest it. Because if the majority of people follow the majority, it is difficult to suggest a different narrative when you are not the majority. But the movements in society are like slow-moving water where, constantly, new waves build up. Different movements get overexaggerated for years, until a new movement arises, which typically exaggerates in the opposite or a completely new direction. Because when water is moved in one direction, it sloshes right back and the water will never be still.

In the movie *The Matrix*, the main character Neo is offered two pills. If he chose the blue pill, he would wake up, forget what happened and live his life as he always has. He chooses the red pill, though, and it makes him find out that his life so far was actually just a computer simulation. Without a doubt, everyone watching the movie likes the fact that Neo takes the red pill. But would everyone watching it have taken the red pill in real life? In reality, most people want to live their normal life and do not see the need to seek and understand things beyond their current beliefs and the mainstream narrative. But maybe you would have taken the red pill. Maybe you are a queen and are willing to take different standpoints and views into account. Perhaps you are one that has tried to not ride with the different waves of society and looks at the restless water from a distant view. But if you have something truthful to say, which does not fit into the mainstream narrative, and if you don't swim on the same wave, you might experience how you swiftly become disliked and silenced. If everyone at the table is against you, it is a simple task for others to discredit anything you say. Unfortunately, when you get discredited by the whole round at the table, it gives the impression that you have "lost" the argument. This gives the impression that because you have "lost" the argument, you are, therefore, wrong. But that is a fallacy. Losing an argument does not automatically mean that you are not right. If there is nobody around who wants you to be right, it is impossible for you to "win" an argument. Just because you are alone arguing and all others discredit you, that does not indicate anything about the validity of what you say. Only, if some people decide to listen to you, will there be a chance to bring forward your ideas or your objective points of view. This is why more people need to use Root Access Life. So they can listen to other perspectives, even if they feel cozy in their current opinions and convictions.

What if you saw an error in the mainstream narrative or in how the mass is behaving? What if there was a mass belief that was actually fatally misleading? Do we have to watch the mass, with its beliefs and moral values, never able to voice a different opinion? Do we have to accept being ridiculed, every time we see things differently?

I am of the opinion that we can make a difference in the world and change it positively, even if a majority of us live by the program of mass dynamics. Let's assume that just 10% of people are open-minded enough to listen to what you have to say. That would include countless people on the planet. Reaching out to all these people will be enough work to start with. We can try to inspire people to use Root Access Life, or we can focus on the people who are already open-minded and willing to see through their programming of mass dynamic. If you feel like the mass is wrong on something, focus on the more open-minded people first and be patient with everyone else. The more people see through an error of the mainstream belief, the more are then again willing to see through it. Because after all, that is how the programming works.

> *The understanding of the mass dynamic can bring you to question one of our most deeply wired programming.*
>
> *Imagine you grew up alone on a deserted island. How would your opinions be different? What are your true personal beliefs, uninfluenced by others and by the trends of a society?*
>
> *This might be incredibly difficult to answer but challenging ourselves with such questions grants accesses to the root.*
>
> *Don't be a pawn on the chessboard of life. Be a queen that can walk freely and independently. Acknowledge the mass dynamics and the effects, good or bad, that it has on you. Challenge mass beliefs, just*

as much as you challenge any other beliefs, before you adopt them.

Beyond Mainstream

One doesn't discover new land without the willingness to lose sight of the shore for a long time. – Andre Gide

As a queen, you can go many steps further than all other chess pieces and you can go on any desired field. That is why the queen is of highest value in the game. Unless you are blocked by other chess pieces, you are able to move freely as a queen. Therefore, you should not get yourself stuck when other players on the chessboard won't move as freely as you. Root Access Life does not mean that our settings have to be completely different or that they all need to be changed in some way. Root Access Life means that we have the capability of changing or understand these settings when necessary. That capability and the awareness of that capability makes us a queen. The queen can stay on one field for a majority of the game, but when the time comes, she can move anywhere. This chapter is meant to inspire you to step further than the majority and to see beyond the beliefs and views of the mass, when the right time comes to do so. That is of crucial importance, because the programming of the mass is perhaps one of the deepest and most hindering codes in our system.

One time, whilst writing this chapter, I ate lunch, consumed with my thoughts on the topics of mass dynamic. The thoughts about our tyrannical behaviors in groups gave my food a bitter taste. However, then I decided to focus on all the beauty in human creation and all the inspiring, wonderful people there are. Right now, I am eating this food that someone grew and harvested, that someone transported to the store and that someone else sold to me. I am eating from a plate, with a knife and fork that had to be produced, in a room with light that had to be invented. Every single day, we use countless technologies and inventions that passionate human beings have created to the benefit of everyone. In many cases, these are systems and products that have been developed over hundreds or even thousands of years. We live in a comfort that is only possible through the hard work, the genius and the progress of our ancestors and our fellow humans. It's easy to be upset about the human race, for various reasons. But, besides all of our stupidity, there are an endless amount of positive and helpful things humans do and have done. Many of them could have only been done through teamwork, through the cohesion of the masses, through passing on of ideas and knowledge. I respect the power of the masses for that and I respect the human race for its complex knowledge and for its passion and compassion.

At the same time, I see that some of the most valuable inventions and even great revolutions started with single individuals who were brave enough to think differently. It is not the masses that invented the light bulb, but the masses helped to produce the light bulb. The few inventors of the light bulb were bold enough to try something that no one had tried before. Bold enough not to listen to all the doubters and to imagine that something was possible, even if nobody believed in it. Some of the most important teachings that brought me further in my life were teachings that I found outside of mainstream advice. Information which I would not get from public school, from the mainstream news or from the mainstream narrative in society. Highly outstanding and most interesting information that I have found was largely unknown by the norm or even blindly criticized. I am talking about lessons and knowledge that only a few wise and open-minded people teach. With openness to learn, with intuition and without prejudgement, we can see beyond what is ordinary. There are endless teachings in this world that can bring us further in life, that can make us happier, more fulfilled, wiser, wealthier, healthier or improve our social life. We all want a good life, yet many are not willing to go beyond what the norm tells them to do. But the ordinary advice gives us only ordinary results. It gives us ordinary problems, ordinary solutions, ordinary friendships, ordinary diseases, ordinary habits, ordinary jobs and an ordinary life. It is normal to constantly chase things we believe we need. It's normal to be unhappy and unsatisfied. It's normal to have diseases and to have problems within family and relationships. It's normal to work all of life in a job we do not enjoy. Nobody who is truly successful with any of these things has only followed the general advice on how to live life.

The general population tends to be so stuck in normality that it cannot imagine that anything else and anything greater and more abstract could be possible. If we never take a step further than the general population, we will never experience what lays within the realm of possibility and what lays beyond the mass belief.

The person who follows the crowd will usually go no further than the crowd. The person who walks alone is likely to find himself in places no one has ever seen before.
– Albert Einstein

There might be areas in your life in which you want normal results and where you don't see a need to go down any rabbit whole. Surely countless ideas, which are disapproved by the crowd, are gibberish or even dangerous. Don't let this chapter make you think that everything should be changed or that nothing the mainstream teaches us is of any use.

If you wanted extraordinary results, however, it would be silly if I told you to follow the ordinary advice. If you wanted extraordinary answers, it would be silly to ask ordinary questions. For remarkable outcomes, we have to be remarkably open to learning and remarkably willing to find different answers and solutions. You have your own intuition and if you are open to it, you will find what really brings you further in life. Too often, we disregard a great idea just because not all of our friends believe in it. We tell ourselves: "If this would actually work, everybody would do it, so it can only be a scam." But is something only a good idea if all of our friends already do it or believe in it? If everyone thinks that way, could there ever be progress, new ideas and inventions? Big changes and breakthroughs can only be achieved through thinking outside of the box.

Let's assume something as little as upright posture or a simple breathing technique could drastically improve our confidence and life quality. Let's assume, with other simple lifestyle changes, we could drastically improve our health and longevity. Most people would think that it sounds too easy to be true and only a couple of people would make the effort to actually do such a practice consistently, although they require very minor effort. If we put forth the willingness to take a couple of small steps outside of the crowd, we can reach new realms. But the crowd does not necessarily want you to live the best possible life or be ahead of it. It wants you to just live a normal life and to fit in. As long as you fit in and are capable of living an average life, like everyone else, you are well accepted. If you go further or think deeper, you become a threat to the crowd because you grow above it.

> *At first, they'll only dislike what you say, but the more correct you start sounding the more they'll dislike you.*
> – Criss Jami, *Killosophy*

Do not be afraid of the judgements of the crowd. All big inventors that brought new great ideas and inventions to humanity were, at some point, doubted, laughed at and disputed by the masses. These people were brave enough to challenge the mainstream beliefs and see new possibilities and truths that no one else was willing to see. Instead of getting praised for new ideas, big inventors were, throughout history, repeatedly labeled as "crazy". If we call people who have abstract ideas for the future crazy, we might as well call every great invention crazy. Of course, nobody can predict the future precisely. Surely, many inventions were luck and a lot of abstract thinkers were wrong with their predictions and unsuccessful with their ideas. And surely many ideas not offend that are outside the box are idiotic. The point is not to believe every new idea or everything that is outside of the box. The point is to listen and study carefully and to at least give new or unpopular ideas a chance. Even if they sound strange at first. Most of the time in history, the popular belief was close-minded towards inventions which we could not imagine to live without today. There was a time where people strongly doubted the invention of cars. They laughed at the idea and predicted that we would always use carriages and horses to drive. Around the beginning of the twentieth century, the first motorized airplanes were about to be invented. Previously, nobody believed that a motorized plane could possibly carry itself through the air and such ideas and inventions got ridiculed. Until their success was absolutely obvious to everybody.

Around fifty years later, fighter jets were capable of flying through the air at supersonic speeds and nobody would put such inventions into question. When the internet came up, people doubted that its usage would ever be widespread. Electricity, the light bulb, television or mobile phones were all inventions that were highly doubted and laughed at by the mainstream society at one point. Yet, having and using these things is unquestionable in the current time. The good news is that doubted inventions can slowly get adopted by more authoritarian people and companies. And after a while, the general news might report positively about them. Then, when everybody talks about it and when the news for the first time talks greatly about these inventions, the adoption by the mass can kick in. As the famous saying by Mahatma Gandhi goes, *First they ignore you, then they laugh at you, then they fight you, then you win.*

History tells us that most people will always be close-minded about new ideas until authority figures, news stations and a larger group slowly accepts them. This shows that early investors, inventors and supporters of completely new ideas were capable of seeing beyond the mainstream view. And they made use of Root Access Life.

Doing something different and swimming against the stream is less predictable and often scary. And sometimes, going an unpredictable path may lead you to an undesired place and away from the comfort of a group. But if we never go there, we will never know. While the standard convictions and advice can oftentimes be enough, we should not forget that the standard advice will only give us standard results. And there are even situations where it can give us the worst results.

When the price of a stock or any asset goes up or is high, most people get hyped-up about this particular investment. The news then talks greatly about it, people consider buying it and they advise you to do the same. When the market is low or drops, the news and the general population will talk badly about this investment and the majority considers selling it. The few people who made the most profit, however, did the exact opposite of the mainstream. They were brave enough to buy an asset, even though there was no hype or good news at that time. And they were brave enough to sell an asset when the news was good and everyone was hyped. These people were willing to thoroughly inform themselves and see an opportunity at a time when only a few were willing to pay attention. There is no guarantee that an unpopular investment will turn out to be great. But it is absolutely guaranteed that following the mainstream buying hype and the mainstream selling fear will give us the worst results for our investments. So, giving up or discrediting something because it is not yet accepted by all of society does not make much sense. It is necessary to swim against the stream at times, especially if we want to end up with an extraordinary outcome.

If you want to have the best possible life, would you mimic the lives of most people? If you wanted to be rich, would you follow general investment advice or work at a nine to five job? Would you spend your money like most people? If you wanted to cure a chronic illness, would you accept taking pills for the rest of your life, as most people with a chronic illness do? You could dig deeper and at least try to find a better solution. A solution that does not just quickly fix the symptoms of a problem, but a solution that tackles the cause of a problem. It doesn't matter whether it is health, nutrition, psychology, finance, relationship or general life advice. With a little bit of interest, some digging and willingness to see beyond conventional teachings, we open the door to deeper insights and we enable the opportunity to be miles ahead of the norm.

Life changing "secret" tricks are usually not handed out to us through the mainstream media. We usually find them if we dig a little deeper and are a little more open to what we find. It does not take a lot to stand out from the crowd and get better results in life. Most of the time it only requires us to be a little more vigilant and to be willing to go just a little bit further into different directions. Every invention has been done by people who thought a little further and went a little deeper than the masses. Every successful person did something that the masses did not do. Only that is why that person is successful in the first place. If everybody did it, it would not be considered success. Yet, the masses live by the belief that if something works and is true, everyone would do it already and if nobody does it, it cannot work or be true. This is the reason that everybody is not an inventor, that everybody is not successful and that everybody does not see all angles of the chessboard.

Most people like to stay in the safe zone. They eat the same foods as everyone around them, they have the same life path and curriculum as their friends and they listen to the mainstream media for information. It seems so safe, but is it really?

Following general dogmas is easy but it is not safe, as it brings normal results, but also normal problems.

Anyone is free to use Root Access Life and see the pros and cons of the general advice. Just because everyone uses electricity, that doesn't mean you shouldn't and just because everyone believes you should brush your teeth daily, that doesn't mean that you shouldn't. Perhaps take the general beliefs and advice as an inspiration and a reference point. From there, if there are any areas in which you want to be better, or if there is any controversy, take a look beyond the general beliefs. By removing ourselves from the mass, the sight clears up from all the dust that the mass stirs up from all the doctrines and convictions it has opposed on us. Oftentimes, life can be much more simple than we think, but it seems very complicated to figure that out.

"If it worked, everyone would do it." This sentence should be changed to: "If you want the results everyone has, do what everyone does. If you want different or better results, you must do something else."

We can choose to take the alleged "safe" route, which will give us mediocre results in life and bring us predicted problems. Or we take the risk to think and look deeper, to theorize more and to discover new land. The problems we will face will be less predictable, but only by taking such risks can world-changing things happen.

Sometimes the best play of a queen is to move in the opposite direction of the pawns. With

Root Access Life, you can question the mass and you can bring up the will to go against the stream, if you truly find it necessary.

If your mind was an operating system, you could choose to ignore your default settings. Or you could choose to access the root and see beyond them or change them.

Ambiguity Tolerance

The test of a first-rate intelligence is the ability to hold two opposed ideas in mind at the same time and still retain the ability to function.
– F. Scott Fitzgerald

How we identify within ourselves and the identification we hold towards the outside world appears to be of immense importance to us. Having evolved in tribes, it makes sense that we know who we are and where we belong at any given time and in any situation. This may have positive or negative aspects to it. A rather problematic part of constantly needing to identify ourselves is the occurrence of constant hostile groups. All too often, we are confronted with opposing stances and people quickly identify with one or the other group in society. You are then pushed, by the crowd, to also pick a side and to fully identify with it.

"If you don't choose left, you must choose right."

"Either you fully agree with what I believe, or you are on the side of my enemy."

"If one side sounds too crazy, then the completely opposite side must be 100% right."

"If you don't go this way, then you must go that way."

These are typical settings in our systems that distance us from seeing the whole spectrum of a subject matter rationally. When we identify too much with one side or one group, it is impossible to be objective. It keeps us from seeing perspectives beyond a two-dimensional, oversimplified world. "One or the other" thinking brings strong tribalism and it distances us from objective truths. But by seeing things in different ways or from different angles, we reprogram our brain to be less dogmatic. Because a dogmatic brain is a chess piece, glued to one field. On the chessboard, there are black and white fields, but the queen can walk on all of them.

Often, there is one public mainstream opinion to a subject matter that we are dared to question. Only a minority hold other, mostly suppressed, opinions. But it is also common that two prominent, opposing masses, with opposing views, form. This is understandable, as humans love to create opponents and draw a bipolar picture. How boring would it be to watch a football game if there is no opponent to be defeated? Just as in sports, the mass dynamic creates such opposing poles in society. Both sides are all too often convinced that their side must be 100% right in every single aspect. And that, in turn, the other side must be 100% wrong in every single aspect. Both sides create their own crowd and their own inner mass dynamic. Our deeply rooted programming, of course, then creates the idea that we are on that right or the "good" side. And that the other side is the ultimate "bad" side. When both sides think they are 100% right and the other is 100% wrong and has absolutely no valid point of concern, conflicts become an endless battle.

Finding fault, pointing fingers and labeling who is "good" and who is "bad" is a way in which groups, societies and cultures make themselves feel morally superior over others.

But things are usually more complex than simply finding another party to blame. And, in most cases, empathetically looking at the other side, we see at least some valid arguments.

When we are part of one society, one country or one group, in a conflict, we only get to hear the "bad" about everyone else and the "good" about our own. Take two countries involved in a war. Mainstream news stations in our country will 100% of the time propagate that our country is the "good" in the conflict. The exact same thing is exclusively propagated in the opposing country. And both countries have a perfect-sounding alibi. Do we really know what is going on if we only see and hear information from one side? Are we perhaps missing a part of the story? Perhaps both countries are "bad". Perhaps both are "bad" and "good" at the same time. Or perhaps one is very "bad" and the other is a little less "bad", but still "bad" nonetheless. Or one is more "bad" in this instance and the other is more "bad" in another. We are not a queen and we are most certainly dominated by our programming if we blindly trust the mainstream propaganda on one side without sincerely listening to the other side. By overly identifying with one side, one team or one origin, we will never see the parts that mainstream propaganda conveniently omits or the parts in which we are misguided by our leaders.

The one using Root Access Life can listen to anyone on any side and see the pros and cons in any aspect. No need to overly identify strictly with one side or one narrative. The one using Root Access Life can see that many stupid arguments on one side do not make the opposing side more valid. We can support certain points on one side and support other points on another side, while seeing the not-so-great points in all of them.

Is "good" and "bad" always 100% definable? The birth of new life is something wonderful, yet it also entails that this new life has to suffer death at some point. Therefore, creating life paradoxically also creates death. You see, our brain doesn't like to live with such paradoxical thoughts. Especially with the idea that some things might be, in a sense, "good" and "bad" at the same time. But in many aspects of life, there is ambiguity. Things can be, in a sense, good and bad at the same time. Two opposing sides can have their valid points of concern. But, unfortunately, only few have tolerance for such ambiguity. And only few seem to be able to hold opposed ideas in their mind at the same time.

We tend to want to see ourselves and the group we chose as the "good" at all times. But when we humans pretend, too excessively, to be on the "good" side, we easily entangle ourselves in our own ideologies. Because whatever is considered to be "good" can also be exaggerated to the point where it shows negative effects. Stealing, for example, is generally accepted to be something rather "bad". Therefore, being anti-stealing must be a very good thing, right? In a crowd with common sense, or in a fair court, the specific circumstances and the severity of a crime play a huge role. Should we lock people up for years for stealing some chewing gum? That would obviously be overexaggerated. But in overly idealistic groups, we are pushed into taking such undifferentiated stances. The programming can be illustrated like this: "You are either anti-stealing or you are pro-stealing. If you are not extremely anti-stealing and don't agree with every punishment against stealing, you must be in support of stealing. Therefore, you are probably even a stealer yourself and certainly, a very 'bad' person." In countless areas, our societies are overly moralizing and tend to push us into such nonsensical constructs. Even simply informing ourselves about different perspectives can quickly make us a target, whether we take a stance or not. But informing ourselves is the basis of understanding. How can that be a bad thing? Every good court will inform themselves about the circumstances and the reasonings of a criminal. Trying to understand motives of a criminal and reasons behind a crime does not make the court sympathize with that crime or support it. A good legal system recognizes that we need to listen to all sides, including the standpoint of the accused. In court, every accused has the right to defend him or herself and explain his or her reasonings. Even the worst criminals are allowed to explain and defend their actions. Does this mean that a good legal system sympathizes with criminals or that they won't punish them? No, but for good reason, every person should have the human right to legally defend him or herself. For good reason, the specific circumstances and the severity play a role in the verdict. Just because you are listening to a perpetrator, that doesn't mean that you sympathize with his or her actions. Just because you try to take different points of view into consideration, it doesn't mean that you agree with any of them. Categorizing and labeling people and behaviors, without the will to thoroughly understand them, creates unnecessary hate and is a toxic behavior. A rational discussion is out of the question if the goal of participants is only to feel morally superior. And the craving of moral superiority leads to irrational, radical and conflicting ideologies. In overly moralistic societies, objective views, rational discussions and pragmatic action become impossible. In order to have a rational discussion, we need to be able to understand different sides. Even if we do not agree with them. We have to be able to live with the fact that many areas of life and many topics are ambiguous. There are not always simple answers to every question. Either "good" or "bad", "yes" or "no", "this" or "that". Sometimes it's "good" and "bad", "yes" and "no", "this" and "that". It's our genetically coded natural instinct that makes us categorize things into opposing groups. But it is often a threat to peace, justice and sanity.

While there are not always strict rules in life, there are certainly tendencies. For example, the "natural" way may not, in every single case, be the best for humans. As it is also not always clear what is "natural" and even what is best for us. But there can certainly be a recognizable tendency. Understanding nature and applying more natural ways of living on this earth tends to be beneficial for human beings and the planet. So it makes sense to see tendencies and it makes sense to have certain guidelines. But there may not be a clear rule for everything, especially when it comes to morals and ethics. People seek ultimate rules to follow or an ultimate group to follow by default, without having to think. There are tendencies, there are exceptions, there are irregularities and there are unexpected surprises. There is not always a clear left or right, up or down, black or white. There are different angles, different views, different pictures. The bishop can only move diagonally on either the black or the white fields. To see the image fully, we have to be able move on all fields like a queen and use Root Access Life in every new situation. The problem with tendencies is that we have to think in order to understand different circumstances individually. Just because there is not always a clear rule, that does not mean that there is no strong tendency. And just because there is a strong tendency, that does not mean there is a strict rule. It is easier to live by clearly defined rules. Our lazy self hates it if we have to think freshly when a similar situation or topic arises. If it is a similar situation, we rather just give it the same name and put it in the same box, without having to think.

"This is bad, this is good, this is wrong and this is right."

"If it's not this way, it's always that way."

Such rules leave us with less to think, but they also shut down the opportunity to see new and different patterns, tendencies and exceptions. Fixated rules and dogmatic categorizing and labeling again makes us close-minded and is a reflection of grayed-out setting. They lead us to either agree on everything a person or group says, does and thinks, or disagree on everything. The socially wired setting goes like this: "If a person says this one thing, he is a bad person and therefore everything else that person says is also wrong and bad." Or: "You either fully agree with a person or you fully disagree with that person." This way of thinking comes in handy when a group tries to discredit an idea. Instead of finding good arguments against the idea, people often try to find arguments against the person. In other words, when they can't beat the argument, they need to beat the person. This is an easy way to win arguments, because nobody likes to believe the one who has a negative label. Yet an idea itself can be great, regardless of who talks about it or of how that person is labeled. If a mass murderer says that it's healthy to eat vegetables, does that automatically make vegetables unhealthy? Surely not. And just because you also think vegetables are healthy, that doesn't mean that you sympathize with this mass murderer. Hippies were against war. Does that make you have to agree with every part of their lifestyle because you agree with their stance on war? Of course not. Unfortunately, discussions can quickly get off topic when the arguments are not about the subject matter but about the identification and the labeling of participants. When we watch any controversial topic being discussed in society, we rarely see a constructive, open discussion between people who are taking different views into consideration or that are trying to find objective and rational arguments. Typically, instead of good argumentation, we hear accusations between opposing individuals and we are pushed into picking a side.

But if we force ourselves to pick an ultimate side, our opinions get more extreme and our reasonings weirder. The hate against the opposing side will push both sides into even more radical beliefs, which rationally do not make sense. The more radical the stances on one side, the more radical the stances on the other side tend to get, into the opposite direction. Psychologically, we tend to lean in the opposite direction the more the other person leans into his or her direction. As if leaning out the rail of a boat, not wanting it to capsize over to the other side. The less the other person is willing to agree with us on anything, the less we tend to be willing to agree. But when both sides get together in the boat, it won't capsize. Only if one stubbornly leans out the rail, the other is forced to lean out in the other direction. This shows when arguments are extremely one-sided and intolerant for any other opinion. Naturally, there will then be people who try to counter-steer and suggest extreme counterarguments. This makes sense to a degree, because it is an attempt to eliminate one-sidedness. And stubborn one-sided thinking is the biggest preventer of Root Access Life. Only if both sides are willing to inform themselves about other perspectives and possibilities can they get back in the boat and prevent it from capsizing. Inside the boat, there must not be an agreement on the subject matter, only a willingness to at least listen to other perspectives.

Perhaps one side can admit that the other is partially right and the other can admit that the former is partially right. Once you look at a topic from more than one angle and research critically and objectively, you will most certainly get a different picture than you had before.

If I said that black-and-white thinking is always radically wrong, that would, in a way, paradoxically, be black-and-white thinking. So let me say that in most areas in life, extreme one-sidedness isn't the smartest. If we are overly nice, for example, we get walked over. If we are overly cool, we miss love and compassion. We can see pros and cons and make use of the benefits of both sides. We can be kind and loving, while having strong boundaries and standing up for ourselves. I assume that you agree that being unnecessarily violent to other creatures is not a sign of greatness. However, even here we could go into an unnecessary extreme. If I forbid myself to walk outside for the sake of not stepping on any insects, the point of being nonviolent is taken too far, in my opinion. Naturally, if all people stay at home for not stepping on any insects, there will be others who protest such radical behavior and perhaps even counter-steer with more violence.

It has to be said that some views might be perceived as extreme, but only because they are unusual. In a time where open executions were normal, radically not supporting them would be considered extreme. Sometimes we may want to strictly defend our views and ethics. Sometimes we have to go to extremes to find a middle ground. And sometimes we go through phases. The difference is whether we consciously choose to see opposing sides and accept ambiguity, or if we get pushed into picking sides like a leaf in the wind.

> *Be aware of how you are pushed into a "one or the other" mindset by society. Don't blindly follow strict rules, pick sides or accept narrow views. Think for yourself and acknowledge that the world is not black and white, but complex and it holds endless shades of every color.*

The Compassion of Groups

> *Murder is the gravest crime man commits; yet war is murder multiplied by the majority. By what ethics, then, is the man a criminal, and the mass heroes?*
> – Ezra H. Heywood

Fitting into a group well gives us a feeling of being on the right side and of being a "good" person. This programming, however, can get very destructive and much evilness arises because of it. If the norm accepts a specific violence, people would not feel bad for exerting that violence. On the battlefield, a man from one side believes he is fighting for a good thing and the man on the other side thinks he is fighting for a good thing. While they are both doing a not so good thing: killing.

We humans are able to turn off our compassion when violence is accepted by the group or society. This is seen throughout countless large tragical events and wars in history. For example, the tragedy of witch burning in the Middle Ages. It was, in many areas of the world, accepted that people would get burned alive if they seemed abnormal or simply if someone accused them of being a witch. Extreme violence was normalized, accepted and supported.

Does this mean that all involved humans did not have any compassion, or that they were all generally evil? No, for most people involved, it was probably their deeply rooted programming and settings that turned off their compassion and inner convictions for what is right or wrong. The code in our system that makes us believe that whatever the norm does has to be right and good turns us evil. Not necessarily our sincere inner convictions. While there is certainly individual evil and psychopathic behavior in this world, the large sum of people appears to be compassionate and protecting at its core. Until the mainstream propaganda creates a scapegoat and the programming of mass dynamic disables compassion.

The dynamics of the mass can make compassionate human beings turn cold and evil. And in the mass, the ethical values of every individual, such as rational, autonomous thinking, can completely vanish. Ideas that the individual would naturally reject may suddenly be fully accepted and defended. But the mass is never evil, aware of being evil. The mass is evil because it is so persuaded to be on the right side and therefore thinks its evilness is actually greatness. Soldiers defend their killing by saying they are just defending their country. Even if they are fighting in a different country. A feeling of fellowship and of being on the "right" side, of allegedly protecting their country, makes killing justified to them. The same soldiers would be against killing if it wasn't for war. They would perhaps be against killing if they knew the enemy personally or if they sincerely talked to the soldiers on the other side. Their own ethical values are not fundamentally for killing, but the mass dynamic makes it OK for them.

When the mass is being steered and manipulated into one direction, there is always a perfect alibi and explanation set in place. "You are a great and brave man if you go to war and fight for your country." You are called a little wimp or a traitor if you don't go to war and kill other men, husbands and fathers. The alibi is that it's all about protecting your own country or group and, of course, that any other country is evil and guilty. If you question that, you are said to be a traitor against your country or your group and, therefore, allegedly supporting the other, evil country. You see, it always comes down to the same concept: you either fit in or you are bad person. Propagandists use this as a tactic, by attacking our deeply rooted fear of being despised by the group. Of wanting to be a good citizen and a good fellow. National propaganda makes the mass hateful against other human beings and national propaganda tells you, that you are a hero if you destroy them.

While this mass dynamic is immensely dangerous, I can, of course, see how it is a natural part of our evolution. And with that, I can see cases where it may be of advantage. Imagine a time, thousands of years ago, when there was no hospital, no police and no court. Imagine another tribe was attacking your tribe to steal all goods and to kill all your companions. Not anything unusual in human history. In this case, in such life-or-death situations, the mass dynamic can build up the strength and the coldness to fight and defend effectively. So having a sense for the group can surely have its advantages. And, most certainly, it was the only way to survive throughout our evolution. That's another point of view we are able to take. It is, however, my ambition to point out the dangers of group dynamics and our automated behaviors, as their negative impact can be so horrendously devastating.

If we try to explain our cold, tribal behaviors through evolution, we may have an explanation for many devastating conflicts created by humans. Throughout evolution, the groups that were very ruthless towards other groups and only compassionate within their own must have been very successful in surviving. This may be why human beings, who are compassionate and vulnerable by design, have the capability to be cold-hearted and evil towards other groups. Compassion, although inside of our hearts, can be turned off, like a button on a mobile phone, as soon as there is an opposing and condemned group. One may be very compassionate towards people within his or her group, but this compassion can be disabled towards members of other groups. Especially when these groups are discredited, blamed and accused.

The mass has compassion, but only towards whomever is part of the same mass and whoever fits in. Every individual, however, has compassion within him or herself. And beneath our programming and settings, we see injustice, regardless of the group we identify with.

With all the violence and suffering humans have caused throughout history, it is easy to think that we humans are generally evil creatures. But I believe that we are not evil killing machines by design. I can say with much certainty that we humans function best within ourselves and together if we try our best to construct rather than destruct, and love rather than hate. This is not to say that violence may never be necessary, or that a feeling of hate could never give us the strength needed to change miserable circumstances. But whenever we exert hateful or violent behavior, we not only risk damaging others, but also ourselves.

Countless soldiers return from war and get addicted to alcohol and drugs or commit suicide. Countless soldiers inject testosterone and take drugs to be tougher. Countless people need psychotherapy after seeing tragic events. If causing and feeling pain was so natural and suitable to humans, why is there such a massive use of painkillers?

Yes, human beings do and have done cruel things. But I believe that we do best if we use this capability only when there is absolutely no other way. We are very clearly designed to want peace, to be compassionate, to reduce suffering and to evolve in a constructive way. We are given a brain to think and a mouth to talk in order to resolve conflicts pragmatically. The destructive forms in which humans live destroy not only other people's lives and the planet, but also the life of the one that exerts the violence. The person who causes unnecessary suffering always reduces his or her own life quality and mental health. The reason why we humans do evil things is, in most cases, not because it corresponds to our best interest, or because it is a wise decision. Most of human violence, so I believe, is created through the programming that is capable of turning off our compassion. A program which I call the programming of mass dynamic.

Remember, that in your mind. you are free and neither propaganda nor group pressures should have the power to disable your compassion.

A SENSE OF ALMIGHTINESS

A queen knows her worth, but she is never arrogant, knowing that she is just as vulnerable as any other chess piece.

One wrong move can make her be captured by a pawn.

When we look into our operating system, we can see how its complexity can easily mislead us. It is easy to make mistakes and it is easy to get influenced by our programming. The one who practices Root Access Life will quickly understand that feeling almighty and arrogant hinders us from truly understanding and learning.

This chapter is meant to inspire you to be humble towards life and open to the unknown.

Life Is a Mystery

The more I learn, the less I realize I know.
– Socrates

Life is magical and if you believe in life, you believe in magic. Without this awareness, you won't recognize a wonder, even if it is right in front of your eyes. The idea of being able to explain everything covers up the mystery that is actually behind things. In an effort to name and explain every organ in our body, we forget that existence in of itself is unexplainable, that wonders like the human body give us every reason to be amazed. We live in a world where everything seems to make sense, while nothing really makes sense. In a world where explanations are limited and unanswered questions are endless. But the uncertainties about existence can fuel our sense of wonder, amazement and humbleness. We do not even know what we are doing here, where we are, why we exist or how something as incredible as the universe is possible. We could explain it through religion, try to explain it with science or not bother to think about it at all. Whatever we like to believe, we all have to admit that the universe, the world and life is a wonder which we will never fully understand. There is no need to rationalize the mystery of existence or to deny the magical wonders of life.

None of us can understand or explain the end of the universe. And if the universe and our mere existence is unexplainable, why would anyone think that everything within it has to be explainable? Not believing in magic has to be just as "crazy" as believing in magic. In a way, we can only accept the fact that we experience this crazy journey called life that we cannot fully understand. All we can really do is marvel at it, the way it is.

Thanks to science, we can assume quite some things about the universe. Some astronomers estimate that there are as many stars as there are grains of sand across all beaches on the world. Every star is supposedly of similar scale as the sun or sometimes much larger. We believe many of these stars have planets surrounding them and billions or even trillions of these stars form a galaxy. There are allegedly trillions of galaxies and going from one galaxy to another would take hundreds of thousands of years, traveling constantly by the speed of light. These dimensions of the universe are mind-blowing and it is astonishing how we invent technology to partially observe the universe. But, after all, its existence remains a huge mystery. Considering all of the miraculous aspects of the universe, it is almost hilarious how humans on this little planet called Earth love to act like they know it all. We like to feel superior to others and to everything that exists. If something seems a little unexplainable, we explain it with so-called science and feel as though we are God.

The belief in God is a great belief, if it helps us to stop playing God ourselves. No matter how pretentiously humans behave, it does not change the fact that the universe and existence is unexplainable and a mystery to all of us.

If you found out that someone lied to your face once, you would probably ask yourself where else that person lied, right? If something so incredible, like the universe, is possible, you could ask where else incredible, unexplainable things are possible. Why would something indescribable not be possible within an indescribable universe? There are occurrences in this universe and on our planet that we are far away from understanding. How can we limit our thinking so much that we discredit anything that is not "proven" by humans yet? It makes sense to me that anyone questioning existence itself must develop a certain awe. A humble feeling of experiencing a wonder, being somewhere in an unexplainable universe, on this magical world, in this fascinating body.

We do not know what is possible in the universe and even on this earth. Anything really is. It may not be likely or plausible, but anything is possible, as theoretically life and everything could simply be an illusion. Again, not that it is likely but possible nonetheless.

Someone born in the hot desert thousands of years ago would call anyone crazy who said there is such a thing as snow somewhere in the world. You, living on this world, calling aliens or life in outer space crazy, are perhaps similarly short-sighted. You simply don't know what lies within the realm of possibilities. No matter who we are, what title we have and how confident we might feel, none of us really has all the answers. None of us knows how the world and the whole universe works. Experts try to make themselves look smart, while they try to explain unexplainable things.

As David R Hawkins puts it: *Their confusion is more sophisticated, wrapped in impressive jargon and elaborate mental construction.*

How does a seed grow into a plant? One might explain how the seed grows into a plant by naming different compounds from the earth, water, the sun or air and different chemical processes.

I am asking again, how does the seed grow into a plant? The question is not what reactions we can observe regarding all these compounds and chemicals. The question is, how does a living plant arise out of a small, solid seed? How does the plant actually grow?

It is something we cannot and will never be able to explain. We cannot explain life and existence. We can only observe what happens and how different compounds have different effects on the plant. We can measure, we can observe and we can study a plant. But the actual growing and living of the plant is something we can only admire, as we can only admire life and existence. Turning water into wine may appear as a miracle. But when a seed turns into a grape tree that forms grapes, is that somehow not miraculous?

We can make a study to observe the effects of a plant extract, but the mere existence of the plant itself is a miracle. The study might give us the arrogance to think we understand the world, while the study is built on something that is not understandable. The study supports a better life and gives us interesting insights, but it does not make us almighty.

Observing things and understanding specific mechanisms into every small detail is obviously very interesting and crucial for our development and progress as a species. We should never forget, however, that we do not understand nature at its core. We can only really observe interrelations of different mechanisms.

Do we understand how our heart beats and keeps us alive? We can observe that our heart beats and we can explain the chain of reactions that cause our heart to beat. Impulses of our brain give a signal through our nervous system to our heart, that causes the heart muscle to contract. We can explain mechanisms in which nerves, muscles and our brain operate. We can measure the impulses and chemicals that are involved in the processes. To really understand something though, we would have to know not only that something does something, but also how it does it and why. It seems that we really only discover what is happening and less how and why it is happening, where it comes from or how it is possible. We can acknowledge that the brain sends an impulse, we can acknowledge that the nerves send the signal and that the heart muscle contracts. We can describe the autonomic nervous system. But that is simply an observation of mechanisms, that in themselves are wonders that we cannot explain. The brain, nerves and muscles are undoubtedly miraculous. They are not invented by humans and they are not fully understood by humans and their genius cannot be replicated by humans. Life cannot be replicated by humans. We can observe isolated functions of our body, but we cannot understand the underlying cause of these functions, which is life and existence itself.

So, how does the heart beat? It pumps through muscle contraction. How does the muscle contract? Through nerve signals. How does the nerve give a signal? Through the autonomic nervous system. How does the autonomic nervous system work? How does life work? How is it possible that a matter lives and executes trillions of functions simply fueled by food, water and sunlight? How is our body created that way? It is created through a seed that formed into a human, in the belly of a woman. How does a seed become a human in the belly of a woman? Where does life come from? Why do we have two eyes and not three? Little kids sometimes ask such endless questions and they often lead us to realize that, at the end of it all, we are not almighty. Which is absolutely great!

The human body is truly magnificent and we can try to learn from it and see how mechanisms work. Imagine a UFO from another galaxy landed on the planet and you were assigned to take it apart and understand how it functions. There would be unknown and unexplainable machinery and materials that are out of this world. You could simply watch how they function, while not knowing how they are possible. In a sense, our body and everything on this world is that unknown object. We can be astonished and try to understand how things work, but we cannot recreate things or fully understand how they are possible or where they came from.

A child might ask, "why is fire hot?". The reality is that we don't know why fire is hot, why we have such a thing as sensation, why wood exists and why it is able to burn. After all, we are not the creators of fire or sensations and we did not decide ourselves that fire is supposed to be hot. We can teach children that it hurts when they touch a flame, but we can't teach them why it is hot. We can teach them a perspective of life that makes them wonder how nature works, humble towards all its miracles. As children, we tend to have a pure interest in the world. We are full of wonder and we are open to learn, to grow and to understand this fascinating world.

Over time we are then programmed to believe that we understand the universe because of the smart-sounding answers we get from our parents or teachers. Over time, we get coded by society and some of that pure, sincere interest and amazement gets lost. If we teach our children the arrogance of being almighty, their fascination for life ceases.

The only thing we require to be good philosophers is the faculty of wonder.
–Jostein Gaarder

No matter how educated and experienced we are, we should never feel superior to nature or so arrogant to lose our faculty of wonder. We might craft an airplane and think we are superior to nature, but the airplane is inspired by birds and you cannot replicate a living bird. An albatross can spend years in the air without ever touching the ground and with minimal effort. No invention built by humans comes close to the genius creations of nature. That being said, we humans are, in a way, nature and all the things we are capable of inventing and producing is possible due to our incredible design. In that sense, we can accept that we are not better than this fabulous nature, but a part of it and this should leave us humble and full of awe.

In the dictionary, I found the word "magic" described as something supernatural. This description literally implies that "natural" is not magic, but "supernatural" is. So, technically, if it does not happen in nature, it is magic and if it does happen in nature, it is not magic.

As soon as it happens in nature, though, it would not be magic anymore. Therefore, by definition, magic could only exist when it does not exist. But life in itself is magical, nature itself is! Just because we are used to it and it is "natural" to us, that does not change its miraculousness. If we grew up in a world with flying unicorns, they would be normal and therefore not "magical" to us. A caterpillar eats only leaves, then it creates a thread to fixate on a flat surface and pupate itself. It can hang pupated without food for up to months, until it turns into a beautiful butterfly and flies away.

If that isn't "magic", I don't know what is.

Who told the caterpillar what to do? It wasn't told that it's time to pupate. Nobody taught the caterpillar how to create such a thread and how the complicated pupating process works. Nature is truly astonishing and people trying to mechanically explain everything in life simply make a fool out of themselves.

There is an endless amount of things we do not know or that can only be assumed. Compared to everything we don't know, there is likely only a very small fraction of things that we actually know. At least, that is what I believe. In any case, we will never really know how existence itself is possible. Once you open your mind towards the wonders of the world, you will start to see them everywhere.

Be open-minded, stay interested, be willing to learn, be willing to go beyond general beliefs and be willing to find unexpected answers. Most importantly, practice humility and humbleness, as the world is a beautiful mystery and full of surprises. Accept that we humans have limited understanding of reality. Marvel at the mysteries of the life, the world and existence.

The God of Science

The most difficult subjects can be explained to the most slow-witted man if he has not formed any idea of them already; but the simplest thing cannot be made clear to the most intelligent man if he is firmly persuaded that he knows already, without a shadow of doubt, what is laid before him.
– Leo Tolstoy

If we take a look back at our life, we will all find multiple areas that we would see and handle differently today. We might regret certain actions or maybe we just think to ourselves with a smile: "I was so stupid back then." The way we thought years ago was different and many of our beliefs and behaviors have changed to a degree. We have learned many lessons over the years and often we can't imagine how we could once be so naive and unknowing. This glimpse of time, however, passes too and soon we will look back from the future onto this moment right now. We will look back and see how much we did not know at this point. How much we did not yet experience and learn. Do we know that we are not being naive and stupid right now or that we won't make stupid mistakes again in the future? Chances are very high that we will.

I can say with much certainty that one day in the future, I will read through this book and see many passages I would like to rephrase. Or perhaps I may even see some things I would write completely different in the future. We can be prepared and give our best, but we should never feel too arrogant in our current state. Until we die, there is always room to grow and there are always chances to figure out that we were wrong. That there was more to know or more perspectives to see.

Similarly, we can look back into human history. There are plenty of stupid things that humans did or have believed. In many ways, we know much better now. So, should we have hubris to think that the human race knows it all now and that we won't make new findings or make new mistakes? That would be pretentious. At any point in time, the human race or societies can make mistakes again in different ways and forms. And we will never reach a point where there is nothing new to learn and discover. It requires a special openness and a willingness to understand our operating system, to see our own errors, not just in the past, but also in the ongoing present.

Are scientists, experts and academics ever programmed? Do they all, metaphorically speaking, use Root Access Life to create studies and form unbiased opinions? Are they capable of re-examining their conclusions and admitting mistakes?

Formal titles make it easy for us to feel almighty and arrogant about our current state. Yet feeling almighty and arrogant is like glue that fixates the queen to one field on the chessboard. She may have all capabilities in her, yet if she feels too arrogant to move, she is of little worth.

We are not almighty, we will make mistakes again and again, as individuals, as the human race and as scientists and experts.

The point of this chapter is not to discredit science, experts or formal education systems. The point of this chapter is to illustrate that what is labeled as "science", "expert opinion" or "official information" should not be overly worshiped or blindly trusted. Just as it should not be disregarded by default.

Logically, we instinctively tend to listen to formally educated experts prior to a random non-expert. But trusting a title is only step one in the pursuit of deeper insights. And there is more than one step to take here, so why stay there? I suggest not remaining at level one. At the end of the day, what is actually being said and done is far more important than the education level of a person. And at the end of the day, what matters is the truth. In further steps, you may realize that the formally educated expert was truthful and correct. Or maybe, in rare occasions, you may find out that the opposite is the case. The point is that it should not be the expertise itself that persuades you, but the actual content of what is being said and what is being done. If we are already overly persuaded by the title itself, the most simple facts cannot be made clear to us if they don't match that setting.

What we should care about is the truth. Science and experts may oftentimes be closer to the truth. But regardless, what counts is still nothing but the truth. Not science and not expertise. The latter are merely tools to get closer to the truth. Yet these tools can be misleading and misused for other interests. The truth itself has no interest, yet human beings do. So, if we worship anything, it should be the truth.

Root Access Life requires that we are open to learn more about this world and it requires the realization that this journey never ends. It is an always ongoing process. We should never feel too cozy in the comfort of our current knowledge, or on just one field on the chessboard. Yet ideologizing the idea of "science" does exactly that. If we are too convinced of knowing already, we shut down our ability to discover new and unexpected possibilities. Humanity will never reach a point where there is nothing new to learn or when there are no new mistakes or flaws to be uncovered. We may want to use the best available evidence or the most respected expert opinions as a starting point. From there, without arrogance, we should be open to continuously pursue deeper knowledge. Humble towards all there is yet to understand.

In some areas, I personally have more trust in experts and in so-called "science", while in other areas, a little less. The reason for this is capitalism.

When we fly with an airplane, for example, we trust the system of aircraft construction and the science behind it. We trust how planes are safety checked, how the crew is trained and how mistakes are continuously studied to further improve the technology. We trust all the expertise, science, studying and experimenting that stands behind such incredible technical inventions. Although unlikely, ending up in a plane crash is, of course, possible. But at least I know for certain that I, as a passenger, am not the only one that is highly interested in the plane not crashing. The airline company wants to be profitable; they want to establish themselves and they want to be a good competition to other airline companies. Therefore, they want me to have a good experience with them. Not necessarily because they care about me personally, but because they care about their own success and image. They need me to fly safely, so they can be successful and make money. If an airline had many crashes, I would not fly with them. You see, in this regard, capitalistic systems work very well, as they lead you to be able to have trust and fly safely. The company follows their own interests and, therefore, they operate in your interest. The same goes for many other technologies, products and services that back incredible science and long-term experience. They are constantly developed and they usually work very well or they get fixed quickly.

In different areas of life, capitalism can make products and the science behind it trustworthy. But in other areas, it seems smart to be more alert and careful. An airplane may be studied and developed to be very safe, but an airline company does not necessarily care about the impact that flying has on our environment. As long as people still use their service and they make money, they are not very interested in offering more environment-friendly flights. That is, at least until the day comes where they receive more money for reducing their emissions. So, if an airplane company was to conduct a study with the conclusion that airplane emissions are not a threat to the environment, it should be natural to be somewhat skeptical. While systems and science, based on profit and power, can work very well in some areas, they can be lacking and are sometimes manipulated in other areas.

If I need to get the brakes of my car fixed, the mechanic is the expert. I would not want to do the work myself if I have no expertise or training in this area. So should I give the mechanic all my trust? Let's say he or she advises me to replace my brakes, stating that they are worn out. But when I look at my brakes, they seem just fine to my untrained eye. Should I stop thinking, because he or she is the expert? Well, the mechanic, or the so-called expert, wants to sell me new brakes, as this is his or her job. So there is a conflict of interest and a bias involved. Perhaps my breaks are just fine for another year or two or perhaps my mechanic is totally right and my opinion is just uneducated.

Independent of the car mechanic being right or wrong about the brakes, it is clear to see that there are important differences between my interests and those of the mechanic. It would not be smart to put all my trust and faith in the mechanic, just for being the expert. Perhaps I would want to go and get a second and third opinion from other mechanics or experts. Maybe the tenth mechanic tells me that my brakes are just fine. Perhaps the last mechanic is the first who is sincere. Or perhaps he or she is the only one that is wrong.

Do you see how capitalism can make some systems more trustworthy and others less trustworthy? When it comes to putting trust in systems, in science and in experts, we can't simply follow a strict programming or strictly hold on to our settings. When we understand the interests of different parties, we can assess the amount of caution that should be applied in every new situation.

An area where a capitalistic system may not always make things more trustworthy is also our healthcare system. The airline company and I sit in the same boat, in terms of our interest in flying safely. But a pharmaceutical company and I do not necessarily sit in the same boat when it comes to wanting me to be in perfect health.

Of course our current healthcare system is a blessing, in many instances. Yet is not the point of this example to tell you about all the amazing benefits of our highly developed healthcare system. They are, in my opinion, very obvious and evident. It has to be pointed out, however, that it would be rather naive to think that its sole purpose is to ensure your best health. Our health is so personal, so unpredictable and so mysterious that we can easily blame our own body, our genes, the unlucky circumstances, if we are not well. Chronic illness can easily be called "bad luck" instead of bad health advice. If a pharmaceutical does not help, it may be called "bad luck". But if it makes things worse, it may also be called "bad luck". If a car starts an engine fire for no reason, it is not "bad luck" but a clear mistake by the car company and they will want to fix the problem quickly. In technical fields, the science may be rather straightforward and there is less controversy. But when it comes to topics like health, there is more mystery and more unexplored matter. In such areas, it is particularly important to be aware of different interests. And it is important not to get arrogant, but to be humble and to search for answers with an open mind.

Among experts, scientists and health organizations, antibiotics are pharmaceuticals that are thoroughly studied and accepted as a treatment. For good reason, as antibiotics can potentially save lives due to their antibacterial effects. The human race can be proud of being able to invent such useful and effective medicine. However, there is a major difference between being proud and being arrogant in our pursuit of knowledge. We should be proud of the things we have already learned and humble towards all the things there are yet to learn.

The use of antibiotics is nowadays so widespread and they are so casually prescribed that I personally know few adults, or even children, who have never taken antibiotics in their life. A large sum of people in developed countries have been treated with antibiotics multiple times throughout their lives, although having never faced any life-threatening disease. This could easily make one believe that the scientific community knows every detail about antibiotics and every single effect it may have on our body. Antibiotics can have possible side effects, of which many are studied, reported and laid out in the package information. They have also been found to lead to the negative antibiotic resistance. But while the antibacterial effects of antibiotics are well studied and comprehendible, I highly doubt that anyone understands the full spectrum of all their potential long-term side effects. Not even health organizations, scientists, doctors or experts in the field. One reason for this bold statement is that antibiotics do not only destroy harmful bacteria, they can also affect friendly bacteria. Friendly bacteria that form the microbiome in our digestive system. While I am neither an expert on antibiotics nor on the microbiome, I can recognize that in order to understand the full extent of possible antibiotics side effects, we would need to fully understand the microbiome. The complexity and all the interrelations of our microbiome, however, are yet to be fully understood. And even among scientists, there seem to be mixed opinions in this field. To what extent it influences us, how an ideal microbiome is achieved or how it exactly looks. If antibiotics have a measurable effect on our microbiome, yet we do not fully understand all interrelations of our microbiome, we cannot allege that we know all possible long-term effects of antibiotics. Particularly the effects it may have on our mental health, long term. Because the connection between the microbiome and mental health is becoming more and more recognized, while we are far from fully understanding it.

It does not seem that we are almighty in this area, as mental illnesses are typically not treated by treating the microbiome. It makes sense not to live in a false sense of certainty and to be open to new discoveries and new possibilities. Even regarding very common treatments. I do not allege that I know if or to what extent antibiotics have an effect on our mental health. But I will allege that also nobody else knows exactly if and to what extent antibiotics can have an effect on our mental health. If a doctor is not aware of all the possible effects of antibiotics, how could he or she be so convinced that it is safe to use them in such excess?

You see, this is how our convictions can turn us blind to very realistic possibilities. The problem is not that we use antibiotics to our best knowledge. The problem is the assumption that our best knowledge is the ultimate, fixed truth. That it is set in stone and that it is perfect. The problem is that pharmaceuticals are prescribed with so much persuasiveness that patients would not dare to believe that there could be more to know about the pharmaceuticals they are taking. In the case of a bacterial infection, it is our personal choice to take antibiotics or to try more natural and "softer" approaches. Both paths pose some risks. The potential side effects of antibiotics, such as the potential of getting worse by not taking them. Whichever we choose, we need to take responsibility over our own life and stop worshiping advice in fields that require more understating. And that require us to be much more open to different solutions.

There is more to know in pretty much every

aspect of life. We are very far as a species and there are many things we have learned through good science. It is foolish, however, to believe that we know it all and that no further research or personal experience will ever change our mind. Whether we are talking about common pharmaceuticals or any other standardized practice in society. We should not think that anything which is accepted today, by experts and large organizations, must at all costs be perfectly understood. There will be a point in the future, when we look back and see plenty of lack and bias in conclusions of experts and scientists of our current time. If we look carefully enough, we will abundantly find them today.

Degrees are well and good, as long as they don't stop others from thinking for themselves. And as long as they don't make the holder of such degrees arrogant and have a false sense of almightiness. Science is well and good, as long as the best available evidence is taken as a foundation on which to improve our knowledge without worshiping what the mainstream news labels as "scientific".

Every single day, thousands of new scientific articles are published in scientific literature. Can anyone possibly read through every single one of them, every single day? Do they all represent the full truth and is each one of them perfectly designed, unbiased and unmanipulated? Is there enough research being done in areas where there is no financial interest? Is anyone truly interested in presenting all significant findings to the public?

The vast majority of people do not care about the actual written studies and the actual science behind what they believe. They tend to care more about what is labeled as "science" by the mainstream media or their peers and authority figures. If we cared about the actual science, we would quickly see limitations and warning signals, as most published studies are funded and performed in the private sector. And mainstream news channels tend to report about selected findings, studies and expert opinions, that will provide themselves more views and that are in the best interest of their sponsors. Did I mention that mainstream news stations are largely owned by companies?

We all have reasons to be skeptical towards medial information, even if it is labeled as "scientific" or claimed to be the most trustworthy expert opinion. And we have all reason to be empathetic towards other people who are also skeptical. This is especially true for very controversial and debatable topics. There is not much debate about how a four-stroke petrol engine works. We can read it on the internet, or ask our local mechanic about it. I do not see many reasons to question the science and expertise behind it. But when more controversial topics arise, even the majority of experts, scientists and specialists will be drawn into a mass dynamic, while forming a politically correct narrative. Should the strategy then be to simply follow the majority of experts, as soon as things get a little controversial? That seems like very pre-programmed thinking.

You see, experts are human beings who want to fit in with their peers. They also tend to assume that the mass of academics has to be right in any case. They want to be accepted and they don't want to be defamed or risk their job by stating an unaccepted opinion.

If you are a scientist that is financially free and independent, you are free in your research and in presenting uncensored findings even about the most controversial topics. But if you are, like most scientists, working for an institution, university, government or company, you have a clear corridor of opinion to follow. You are free to present varying research within that corridor. And that research may very well be of a high standard and significant. But when scientists research outside of the corridor and voice a different opinion to controversial subjects, they get in trouble with their employer. They will be bullied by their colleagues, the public and the media and they will get fired.

Not only does the political correctness and the ideology of a society affect individuals, they obviously also affect large institutions and universities, as they are made up of humans. One university does not want to be the black sheep that voices a not so politically correct opinion. So they have to operate within the given corridor of a narrative and ideology. And they make their experts comply.

I give all this criticism because it is worth aspiring to a world where scientists are able to study without limitations and are able to present findings to the public without having to fit into any frame. A world where science is used to gain truth, not to gain money, power or arrogance. Science itself also has nothing to do with fitting in, political correctness, feeling superior or with ideologies. These things should have absolutely no influence on any scientific finding.

Good scientists are interested in what is yet unknown and in new information. Even if that information is contradictory to what they already believe. They acknowledge that there is always more to learn and uncover. Even in a society that pretends to be almighty. Wise are the scientists and experts who confront every topic with a humble, sincere interest to learn more about this fascinating world. They are not only interested in the subjects that are very evident, but especially in those where more evidence is needed. Such scientists are not the people who will always conform to the masses. They are not the people who will always tell you what you would like to hear, what is popular or in their own interest. Their findings may not always be liked by the public and they might even be despised because they look closely at all sides of controversial topics. The real "in your face" truth we get from those experts, who might not be as respected by the mainstream but who are very congruent, honest and frank From those who think independently and who are financially independent. They even speak the truths that infuriate the public and the truths that do not benefit companies, organizations and governments. Because a great scientist, expert or specialist is willing to give up all good reputation for truth.

The only thing a scientist should be interested in is the truth. As the only thing science is intended to do is show us more truth. If he or she is interested in anything other than the truth, he or she is simply not a good scientist.

Understand that science is a useful tool, but it should not lead to blind trust, arrogance or a feeling of almightiness. Don't be overly convinced of knowing already what lays before you, as there is aways more to discover, learn and reexamine.

Science Without Sanity

The only person who is educated is the one who has learned how to learn and change.
– Carl R. Rogers

Human beings have an extraordinary ability known as "sanity". No machine or computer can replicate this unique human quality. At the point a computer is programmed, sanity is impossible, because everything the machine does is based on code. Artificial intelligence uses data, not sanity. To think independently and logically is something very exclusive to us humans. Strictly programmed thinking can have advantages, as it is fast and effective. But it is only the sane mind that can make sense of findings and calculations. No matter how developed computers get, and even if they have their own sort of "mind", their decisions are always traced back to how they are coded by humans. As you have learned, we humans too can be programmed. But unlike computers, underneath our programming, we find logic and sanity. And the way to get there is by accessing the root of your core system.

Fast and effective computers, quantum computing, artificial intelligence or robots are exciting. Common sense, on the other hand, seems to be boring because we are used to it. "That is *just* common sense," one might say. But our sense, whether common or not, is what makes us humans so special and what gives us such great power. Only through our abilities could computers be invented in the first place. Deep in our operating system, past all programming and settings, we find an incredible strength that is gifted to us humans. It is the ability to think independently, extraordinarily and creatively. Science cannot replace sanity but "science", as we refer to it, is a tool that our mind can make use of. While sanity is not clearly definable, it is essential for all great findings, all science, inventions and breakthroughs.

When logic is downplayed and data, numbers, and codes are touted, we forget that data itself is worth nothing without our sense and with the brain that makes use of that data. Knowledge can come from books, teachers and experts. But it can only be turned into wisdom through our own observations, experiences and impressions.

While individual experiences and impressions may be valued too little by society, they are what actually bring forth our ingenuity. If we want to develop our intuition and wisdom, we have to be confident enough to listen and pay attention to the sanity that lays beneath all programming.

You might say that a parachute prevents a person from dying when jumping out of a flying airplane. However, one could argue that there is no evidence for such a claim. Randomized placebo-controlled trials are considered to be high-standard studies in the hierarchy of evidence. Never has there been a study supporting the claim that parachutes could save someone's life when jumping out of a flying airplane. There has never been a study that let some people jump out of an airplane without a parachute and some with a parachute, to then see who survives. That would obviously be unethical and our inner wisdom and logic tells us that it would be unnecessary. Even if there were such studies, there wouldn't be any randomized trials. Meaning that after the test we took the group without a parachute and gave them a parachute to try the same thing all over. If I was very annoying, I could say: "Anecdotes are not proof, only randomized, placebo-controlled studies matter, and therefore parachutes do not safe lives of skydivers." Do you see how nonsensical it can get if sane thinking is discarded?

There is no use of any study or any scientific argument if there is no human sanity involved. In this case, I used a very obvious example to illustrate a point. But in any other, less obvious scenario, it is even more important to use human sanity. Some studies might be not so well designed and without a huge number of participants, but they can still give us a strong indication and spark our interest to further investigate. A computer will see a too-small or badly designed study. But a computer has no passion and no human logic. Studies themselves are just pieces of paper or electronic data. What matters are the brains who made the studies and the brains of those who read them. What matters is our interest to learn and to use all of our deep, inner wisdom to improve our knowledge.

We can put such immense focus on a specific finding or study that we drown in information and lose sight of the bigger picture. We can specialize so much in one area of life that we see the whole world only through that lens. Although great achievements are made through specific expertise, it seems to me that the bigger picture can get lost in the process. It is easy to overly focus on details of our expertise while forgetting to see things with more distance. It is easy to drown in information while neglecting our inner wisdom, sanity and individual knowledge.

> *We are drowning in information but starved for knowledge.*
> – John Naisbitt

When we stand too close to the picture, we don't notice the big elephant. On the other hand, of course, if we stand too far away, we overlook many details. To get the most accurate picture, we have to apply movement and look far, close, left right, up, down.

There is no way to get a clear picture if we are static. What makes our mind so special is this ability to create multidimensional, complex pictures in our head. Numbers, data and scientific findings are great, but what is much greater is our mind, our sanity and our ability to see things with distance, then from up close, from different angles or even through different eyes and with empathy. The ability to put ourselves into different shoes and feel compassion is nothing a computer could apply.

Without human sanity and our ability to apply movement, like a queen, we cannot make good conclusions or good studies. Sanity is the basis of every good study and the ability to see things objectively and from different angles is the basis of every good conclusion.

Can we be academically intellectual and behave stupidly at the same time? Stupid is not the person who doesn't know much, stupid is the person who is convinced of knowing it all. It is not very smart to be close-minded about anything that doesn't fit into our belief system. Or towards anything that is not yet thoroughly studied. Yet academic degrees do not prevent us from being close-minded towards beliefs that do not match our current belief system or ideology. Our opinion is of little use if we are incapable of questioning ourselves and the politically correct narrative of a society. Our titles and our education don't bring truth if we are incapable of taking an objective look at counterarguments or at our opponents' points of view. Our titles and our education don't bring truth if we feel the desperate need to be politically correct, to conform and fit in. Academic degrees do not automatically make us objective, logical thinkers.

We can study philosophy at a university and learn about every philosophy and every philosopher in history. But will that automatically make us great philosophers ourselves? Perhaps we are forgetting that many of the famous philosophers we learn about never had an academic degree in philosophy. So, use your academical intellect together with your sanity, logic, your ingenuity and your inner wisdom. Use studies and teachings of schools and universities to constructs a fundament to further build upon. Because schools don't create genius inventions, they don't seek to find truths to controversial topics and they do not teach what is completely new and unknown. Only brave, independent and logical thinkers do that.

In an established schooling system, you learn what is politically correct and what conforms to the mainstream narrative of a society. So be smart and learn from school just as much as from everything else in life. Be the person who also learns the lessons that school was not able to teach. The lessons that were too controversial or too taboo to discuss in the classroom. The student who believes only what school teaches and disputes everything that is outside of the box, functions well in a career and perhaps even in an ordinary life overall. But he or she will not be the next Einstein and he or she will not find unconventional truths. Someone who learns and executes the orders of our social and educational system well and precisely can be of high value. This ability makes a person skillful. However, what makes us wise is our will to find truth and to use the human sanity beneath all our programming.

> *Wisdom and knowledge are not about how much information you put into your brain. It is a lot more about how you process that information.*
>
> *Process information with sanity and your inner wisdom.*

Chain of Authority

> *Blind belief in authority is the greatest enemy of truth.*
> – Albert Einstein

On the chessboard of life, would a queen follow the lead of the other chess pieces, or would she watch the game unfold and find her own way?

In a nearby city of mine, a house started burning in the city centre and a large group of people crowded around it. Many were curious to see the tragedy and even started to take videos to share on the internet. Allegedly, none of the bystanders felt responsible to call the firefighters. So it happened that the videos of the fire were on social media platforms before anyone had made an emergency call. Regardless of how this scenario exactly played out, the described course of events is very comprehensible. We tend to not feel obligated or responsible to call an emergency operator when so many people are already present. We assume that, obviously, someone else must have already called-in the emergency. If there was only one person seeing the fire, that person would certainly feel more obligated to immediately take action. But in a crowd, we assume that there must be someone else who took the lead already.

You see, it is not much different when it comes to what we believe and what people and information we trust. We like to be lazy and follow leaders. We like to assume that someone else must have done the work we don't want to do ourselves. If everyone believes something, someone must have carefully checked all the reasonings, all the science, the numbers and arguments behind it, right? Well, just as with the example above, more people believing something could ironically mean that less people have actually reviewed the information. When authority figures and a large sum of people believe it, we tend to give away the responsibility and we tend to assume that someone else must have done the work perfectly.

There are incredible authority figures and leaders in this world. People that have spent a lifetime practicing, studying and improving their individual skills. They can have great knowledge and they can have a positive impact on the world. However, trusting authority figures and leaders without being 100% aware of the pitfalls that this trust can bring may be worse than not trusting them.

I don't see a problem in looking up to authority figures. But the deliberate conviction that, without question, these authority figures must be 100% right is rather dangerous. Leaders are not gods; they are human beings. And human beings make mistakes, have egos, personal interests, biases and agendas. Your leaders can be influenced by the same programs and social settings as anyone else.

For some people, their leader is a spiritual guru or the head of a sect. Others follow their famous idols. For, again, others, their authority is the government, official entities and the mainstream media. Some leaders are better than others, but if a leader ever makes a mistake or is corrupt and manipulative, more people follow along. If all leaders across the world were right ninety-nine times out of one hundred, when we give them all of our trust, this one time that they are wrong could be fatal. If 99% of all governments, official entities and official media channels were sincere and unbiased, that 1% would be fatal. Dictators are not a threat; people blindly following dictators are the threat. Propaganda is not a threat; people blindly following propaganda are the threat. Governments demanding war are not a threat; people blindly following that demand are the threat.

In sports, there are always people who are better trained and more skilled in one game or in a specific exercise. Their results are clearly measurable. Someone who has never trained to do a high jump has no chance in challenging the world champion in high jumping. It's very simple: if you are not trained at jumping high, you will not be able to jump as high as the best high jumper.

The same concept, however, does not apply when it comes to logical and autonomic thinking. Everybody has the right and the ability to think logically and critically. Some are very well trained in a specific field. But the ability to think logically, critically and to ask important questions is not exclusive to trained or talented people. When authority figures talk, it may at times seem as if all sanity in the world is theirs and that they own it for themselves. But sane thinking is a gift which is given to us humans and which we can all use freely. We should apply it with humbleness, general curiosity, sincere interest and without prejudgement. But most importantly, we should apply it.

Our initial thoughts may naturally be that, in order to get good information, we should always turn to experts in a field. This makes a lot of sense at first thought. But only as long as it does not blind us. Whatever turns off our ability to think autonomously and individually should be addressed and well examined. Because if everybody lives by the rule of trusting authority, this leads us up a chain which I call the chain of authority. If we ourselves have low authority in a field, we may hang ourselves on another chain link that hangs on another, that hangs on another. At the top, the whole chain is hanging on just one single chain link. The word "depending" comes from the Latin word *dependre*, which means "to hang down" or "to hang from". When we think independently, we do not hang on another chain, but if we depend our entire world view on authority figures, we literally hang on the chain of authority.

A dentist can be an authority figure that people come in contact with and that they trust in terms of their dental health. The dentist has his or her training and experience. But he or she also has authority figures. Perhaps the more experienced coworkers, the professor at university, the chef of the clinic or a big health organization. Who is the authority figure of that dental health organization, for example? Perhaps they get their funding from big investors or companies of which their authority figure might be a few people or a single person. Does the dentist perfectly factcheck every bit of information that comes from above? The information he or she receives may be perfectly correct. But it is often still trusted without question.

So it happens that a whole chain can hang on just the last chain link. Often ending with a few people that have immense power. Anyone can imagine how this hides potential dangers. The more power that is bundled to a few people, the easier it is for them to control, manipulate and follow their own personal interests. The chain link that holds the chain controls what it carries. If one chain link is weak, anything that is attached below it is in danger of falling. So you should not attach your whole world view and all your beliefs and convictions on an authority chain. Unless you yourself regularly monitor the strength and validity of the chain that you are hanging on.

It is smart to test leaders and authority figures with difficult questions if we do not want to be blinded by their authority. Do they respond with generic answers? Are they capable of talking rationally about controversial topics? Do they perpetually side with the narrative of a group? Do they simply comply with what the public or their commissioners want them to say? Do they get mad if we ask critical questions?

At the point where we are not allowed to ask our spiritual guru or the head of a sect sincere and critical questions, we can guess that there is perhaps something fishy. If we are all sincerely interested in finding truth, we would want to question our authority figures and they would want to answer our questions. No matter how uneducated these questions might be. The problem arises that we feel ashamed for questioning leaders. When others around us fully trust them, questioning leaders would make others feel offended. They themselves trust that leader blindly and they do not want to be shook within that trust. If anyone questions their leader, they themselves feel questioned. But questioning literally means that we ask questions and not necessarily that we attack or doubt that individual as a person. As long as we ask sincerely and with general interest. As long as we ask because we want to know more and because we do not want to believe anything blindly.

A bad leader commands, does not accept questions and uses his or her followers to discredit anyone who has different views. A good leader inspires the people around him or her and has an authentic, thoughtful answer to questions. A good leader admits if he or she does not know. A good leader does not try to find fault, but solutions and answers. Most importantly, however, a good leader encourages individual and critical thinking.

He or she wants you to think for yourself, grow wiser and use Root Access Life. While a not-so-good leader wants to control and program you. Good specialists make suggestions and recommendations based on their best knowledge and wisdom. They will be there to help you make an informed decision, but not to make the decision for you. If experts or leaders have a good answer to your question, they should tell you with patience and with kindness. But if the answer communicates something along the lines of "you are stupid, don't question me, I'm the leader", then you know that something is fishy. And that the person is likely more interested in his or her authority than in bringing you the unfiltered truth. If you are pushed into feeling guilty for asking questions, be alert.

With the internet, we have almost unlimited information, accessible just a fingertip away.

Theoretically, we can find almost any documented information in the internet or libraries of the world. Any information that is taught in the world, we could theoretically teach ourselves. Yet this chaos of information can be so overwhelming, that it's easier to simply trust what is on the news, or what authority figures tell us. We live in an age where there is not only more knowledge than ever, it is also more accessible than ever. But the amount and the accessibility alone does not make us automatically better informed. Much rather, this overwhelming amount of information can confuse us even more. If we have no access to information, we can easily be manipulated. But all the information in the world does not change that if we disregard any information that is not approved by our preferred authority.

> *There are great and wise leaders, experts, specialists and teachers in this world. Ask sincere questions and be skeptical of their authority. Not because you want to disrespect them, but because it needs to be done. Acknowledge that our authority figures can be just as influenced by programming, as anyone else.*
>
> *Use the knowledge of Root Access Life, to think autonomously.*

Nothing New Under the Sun

Those who cannot remember the past are condemned to repeat it.
– George Santayana

As we know, a queen can see different angles of the chessboard. But for the best possible move, it's also important to analyze past moves and possible future moves in the game.

Two hundred years ago, people said: "We have the most modern technology, the best laws, the best experts." Today, in this moment, people also say: "We have the most modern technologies, the best laws and the best experts." But even these laws, these technologies and these expert opinions will soon no longer be modern, because time flies with every breath. What is modern now will soon be outdated. Unfortunately, this feeling of modernity and progress tends to make us live with a false sense of omniscience. It creates a feeling of superiority over the people and experts of the past. In some areas, our knowledge is indeed superior compared with the past, but this exact moment is also the past in the next second. So what is right and wrong and what is ethically correct or incorrect should not be measured on the time we live in or on how up to date we feel. It should not be influenced by the trend of the current time.

Laws are obviously important and they can be considered somewhat fair in most modern countries. But laws have always been changing throughout history and throughout different regions. You might find it strange that in another country you can be sentenced to death for possessing small amounts of illegal drugs. Someone else might find it strange that the law in your country allows the slaughter of cows.

The programming of mass dynamic can make people opportunistically follow whatever is the law and the trend of their culture and their current time. When we hop through tragic events in human history, we will see the same pattern of how this works: "If the norm or the law of the current time says it's right, then it is right."

But since the law has always been changing, have we humans also changed at our core? Actually, the rooted programs and settings are still the same. But instead of standing behind the laws and norms of the year, let's say, 1723, people obviously now stand behind the laws and norms of the current time. But not only that, they will gladly admit that the laws and norms back in 1723 weren't ideal. What about the laws and norms thirty years from now? Will the same people adjust and suddenly disagree with the laws and norms we have today? You see, things have slowly changed and will slowly change, but sadly not so our operating system. We are still convinced of our moral omniscience in the current time.

What if, thirty years from now, it is illegal to kill cows for food and they get the same status as dogs? If it was the new norm and law, people and societies would, after a while, accept it and, in fact, they would start to agree that people who eat cows are very bad people. Just as people who eat dogs today. But would people stop eating pigs or chicken? Probably not. Because, in that example, the new law was only forbidding to eat cows. If, suddenly, the new mainstream was to stop eating pigs, people would agree that eating pigs is evil while still eating chicken. The rationality behind it matters little to our operating system, because as long as it is the current law and norm, the programming insists that it has to be right.

It does not matter what your stance on eating animals is and it is not the point of this example. However, it is the perfect example to illustrate how Root Access Life works. A person who uses Root Access Life can see injustice and think autonomously, regardless of the current laws and norms.

Don't wait until the law and the norm changes and start being a queen today. Take a look back at events in history. Take a look at kingdoms and at leaders who used their power to create violence, executions, persecutions and other tragedies. Take a look at what the vast majority of people in the past believed and who they followed. Very likely you will not side with many of their choices. Although we find many things in history cruel and horrific, the masses at that very time would largely agree with it. Masses of people would, in the past side, with what is now considered cruelty and injustice. Today, we tend to often side with the minority or with the outcasts of history, with those who were in the past despised and less so with the masses.

Imagine one hundred years from now, looking back on all tragic political and social events occurring today. Would people side with the masses or would they side with a minority of the current time? Would they side with the outcasts, just as you may side with the outcasts in past tragic events?

One thing is for sure: people from the future will probably not automatically side with what the masses are doing right now. Maybe the outcasts of today turn out to be the heroes of tomorrow. Not anything uncommon in history. When will humans see that a similar type of evilness builds up again and again through the same old programming, through a stubborn conviction of the current norm and an unwillingness to see patterns that have repeated themselves many times in the past.

Feeling modern, almighty, at the front of time and superior to the past can induce that these same old patterns repeat themselves over and over. They repeat themselves without any alarm bells ringing in people's heads. Greed for money, power and control are motives that have always been a driving force behind unnecessary tragedies. Still, such motives often don't seem to alarm the masses when they appear again today. As long as it is the latest news, it must be the best, modern knowledge and therefore "right", so people think. Disregarding old humanly patterns, such as lust and desire for power, money and control.

In movies and history books, we see evil, greedy leaders and we assume that lust for power is always very obvious and always manifests in the exact same ways. But manipulative, tribalistic, power-driven systems can easily be adjusted to the modern day and age. They can look shiny and sophisticated, while concealing the same old threat. They can claim moral superiority, while pushing us into the same old patterns. Human beings and our main drives have not suddenly changed in the modern age. What has changed are the different ways in which we exercise and display those drives. The urge of people to follow the mass and to fit into the mainstream system shows in all kinds of ways and is covered by all kinds of names. Centuries ago, blindly following the mass would look different to what it does today. Yet the programming and the behavioral pattern is still the same. So the same patterns show up again and again in a new disguise and in forms that are adjusted to the modern mainstream narrative.

History doesn't repeat itself but it often rhymes.
– Mark Twain

Only when individuals break free from pre-installed programs and settings can old patterns dissolve. Our instinctual coding, such as wanting to conform to the mass, is not influenced by the time and place we are born in, or which religion or ideology we follow. Even the idea of ethical correctness can be used by the mass to pressure people into blind obedience. A pattern from the past can repeat itself in a more sophisticated, harmless-seeming way and the norm will not recognize that it poses the same problems. When we make a connection, however, and when we try to show the crowd potential repeating patterns, we quickly get interrupted. "That is something completely different, it cannot be compared." Yes, of course it's something different and of course we shouldn't equate past tragedies to current ones. But doesn't it make sense to compare old behavioral patterns with new ones, in order not to make similar mistakes? The mass thinks: "No, because today we are so modern, so developed, so omniscient, under no circumstance compare it with past failures, because today we are superior to the past." So it happens that these patterns can be repeated endlessly, newly disguised, adapted to the modern world, but with a similar basic principle and a similar key message. And anyone who tries to show a connection from past behavioral patterns to present behavioral patterns will be despised. Will tragic past events happen one to one again in the future? Probably not. Yet such events teach us a lot about human psychology and our programming.

One day as a child, I came home from school and told my father about the history class. Shocked about the tragedies, wars and all the evilness of humans, I said to him, "People were so evil, but this would never happen again today." My father responded, convinced that humans are still the same and people would behave the same way. I heavily disagreed, arguing that we are so much further and different now. Yes, we are further and today I am still convinced that the same tragedies would not happen again in exactly the same way. But I am now certain that the same patterns and similar types of behaviors could. They could happen again, in slightly different manifestations and no one would notice that the root cause was the same. As the code that runs and controls us is still the same.

All the fundamental lessons you need have already been learned in the past. All the fundamental mistakes you can make have already been made. The world changes but the same patterns of human behaviors show up again and again in new disguise. Look back at history and learn its lessons.

ACCESSING THE ROOT

To succeed in life, to be fulfilled, happy, healthy, wealthy or even to simply get through life, we are required to learn many lessons. From day one, we learn about the actualities of this world and we are challenged in understanding many aspects of life. Whenever we learn, there is the question of what is the best way for us to individually do so and what information is actually true. The question of how to live life, what to believe and what information is true or false has brought plenty of conflicts and wars in human history. Finding a way through the endless information and possibilities in life and managing our wants, needs and biases can be a massive challenge. This chapter is not meant to give you the lessons. It is meant to inspire a better way of finding the truth for yourself, within the mayhem of information.

Seeking Truth

No one is more hated than he who speaks the truth.
– Plato

One of the most important attitudes we must have, in order to find meaningful answers, is the acceptance of the truth as it is, not as we would like it to be, or how well it fits a narrative. The question we have to ask ourselves is not only what the truth is, but primarily if we genuinely want to know the actual truth. When we genuinely want to know the truth, we are already halfway there. Two opposing parties may have a different idea of what the truth may be. But if they both sincerely want to know the truth, they already have the most important part in common.

There are enough topics in this world to be confused about and the underlying truth is often hard to grasp, or not to find at all. Yet, the approach we should take is always the same; we have to be willing to accept the truth whatever it might be and whether we like it or not. The world offers a lot to learn, but information is only of value if we want to see it, if we have a burning desire to grow wiser. In every new situation and with every new question, we can always ask ourselves: "Do I want to see the truth as clearly as I possibly can, or do I just want to be right?"

This naturally brings up the question, whether there is one ultimate truth or whether truth is just subjective. Is the truth a matter of perspective and how we feel? Are there multiple truths to every aspect?

If I would say that there is never one ultimate truth and everything depends on perspective, that would sound nice to many people and would perhaps be well accepted. It would be one of those nice-sounding answers many people like to hear. Of course, in regard to feelings and emotions, we all respond differently. Our feelings, perspectives and opinions are based on our personal experience in life and we should all be able to feel or think however we want. So yes, our opinions and our feelings can vary, but the underlying truth is simply what it is. There is even a truth about how we feel. Everyone might feel different about the same thing, but then the truth would simply be that everybody feels their own specific way. If you are angry, then the truth is that you are angry. If you say you are happy, but you are actually sad, then the truth is that you are saying you are happy while actually being sad. Or maybe you feel a feeling there is no word for. Then that may be the truth. Our feelings, the world, the universe and everything that exists, including all our opinions and emotions, simply are the way they are and that is the ultimate truth. Whether we know it or not. Logically, there is an ultimate truth to everything, it is just not as simple as we would like it to be. It is not a clear simple truth, but a complex one, that we humans can't always grasp. We can, however, go looking for truth, accepting that there is always more than we will ever know.

The truth could be that there are different sides to a story and that all sides have their own truth, their validity, their tradeoffs, their pros and cons. Especially when it comes to ethical questions regarding good or bad, right or wrong, it isn't easy to have clear conclusions. In that case, the truth might be that ethical conclusions are not always easy to make and that there is no clear good or bad in every scenario.

In my time at school, a teacher once showed us students famous ambiguous images. These show drawings designed to portray two different, recognizable images. Depending on how you look at them, you might see one image or the other. My teacher concluded that these pictures demonstrate how there is no right and wrong and that everything depends on perception. I would argue today that both perceptions are true to the observers, but they do not reflect the full, objective truth. Our perception might be different, depending how we look at the picture, but the reality does not change. The reality of it being a picture created to portray two different images.

One might argue that he sees a face, the other that she sees a vase. But both are not seeing the full truth. Perhaps they are also missing other images that are also drawn into the picture. In a sense, it would be wrong to say that this is a picture of a vase, just as it would be wrong to say this is a picture of a face. The whole truth can only be seen if we are taking different angles and if we are willing to try and see another picture. The truth, however, is independent of how people perceive it. In this case, the truth might be that this is a human drawing, which is intentionally or unintentionally designed so most people are able to clearly see two different images in it. Maybe someone sees a completely new picture in it. In that case, the truth is that most people see one or the other image, while some see two different images and, again, others see something completely different. However the world is looked at, it does not change the fact that it is how it is, detached of how we perceive it or what our opinion about it is.

While the opinion of the majority is driven by convenience, good news for bad habits, egoism, fear and addiction, the reality is not. The truth does not have feelings or morality. It is not attached to correctness, the narrative of a society, beliefs or religions. The truth may often be uglier and less reputable than a society wants it to be. Societies are driven by ideologies, but reality does not care about ideologies. If reality is a cruel, messy paradox, it is just as true, no matter how much we build an ideological narrative around it.

Many truths are never even mentioned or are never of any discussion because they do not fit into popular ideologies. Simply considering them would make us labeled a "bad" person and despised by society.

A lot of people want to know the answer as long as the answer fits into their current way of thinking. So they are longing for the truth, but when you tell them the uncensored truth, they don't like it. If you say what society likes to hear, you will be loved. If you tell something that goes against the general belief, you will be hated. Because the masses would often rather accept a lie than to accept a not so politically correct truth.

We might want to be careful how we address uncomfortable truths, but we should never compromise them for political correctness. If you want to know the truth, be open to finding it, no matter where it might be and no matter if it is less shiny as you would like it to be.

If there is an ultimate truth, how can we be sure that we know it? Is it even possible to understand anything in life fully?

Maybe this life is just an illusion, like in the movie *The Matrix*. Maybe everything is just a dream and we will wake up to find a completely different reality. When it comes to finding truth, we should be able to accept that we do not have to know it all and that we cannot know it all. One of the wisest things we can say is: "I am not almighty and I do not know for sure, I can only make assumptions based on the best of my knowledge."

If a topic really tickles us, if we really feel a desire to know more about it, then we should dig into it and go down the rabbit hole, always aware that we can never know absolutely everything, no matter how many hours we spend learning. If we do not feel the need to go down the rabbit hole, we can simply let a topic be as it is, without taking a radical stance. We do not need to take a certain stance on every single topic. We can simply leave a topic open-ended for the moment. Not instantly taking a stance on a new and trending topic may appear uneducated to others, but it can be extremely wise.

Yet, can we be trustworthy if we are not 100% sure of what we are standing behind? Yes, we can voice our opinion with authenticity. We can say that, to our best knowledge and to all understanding we have at this moment, we stand behind an opinion, while acknowledging that it is an opinion, not necessarily the ultimate truth itself. I ask you, how could we ever be trusted if we are overly persuaded to be 100% right? No matter how convinced we are, we can admit to ourselves: "I could be wrong". Or we can simply listen to someone, without taking a stance or instantly believing that person.

When we say, "I don't believe that person", it is generally understood as, "I am convinced that this person is wrong, or that the person is lying and I have a different opinion". But we can indeed "not believe" someone, while not having formed a strong opinion yet. We do not have to decide between fully trusting or fully disagreeing. We can simply take in information, without taking any stance on it right away. This is a skill that seems simple but is rarely put into practice.

It is not easy to filter information, to find the truth beneath all the conflicting advice and different opinions in this world. We all fall into similar traps again and again and we tend to adopt common beliefs and biases easily. Nevertheless, we can be patient with ourselves and continuously remind ourselves to apply critical thinking. Those who come closest to the truth and have the most objective perspective are not the ones that are perfect, but the ones that can see their imperfections. There will always be the chance of us being wrong and of trusting the wrong person and advice. This should not hold us back from having a strong opinion, but it should hold us back from forming this strong opinion too quickly and naively.

At this point, you might be wondering how to even start the search for truth. After all, there is an endless amount of information out there and we are constantly bombarded with conflicting opinions and advice. How do we go about finding truth if the topic at hand is complex, controversial and difficult to see through?

With Root Access Life, we can understand our settings and we can acknowledge how they steer us towards a belief. Knowing this, we can actively choose to start off by sincerely researching the exact opposite of what we like to believe or what we intuitively believe.

Doing such research does not make us contradictory, it makes us smarter and wiser. A queen naturally wants to research the opposite of what the mass uniformly believes and fails to put into question. If there is any controversial topic we want to know more about, we should go down the rabbit hole. We should dig into it, have a very close look and try to take even the most unpopular and most despised perspectives into account. We should research opposing views sincerely, without cherry-picking or ripping ideas out of context. If, at the end of our search, we decide to keep our initial and intuitive stance, that is absolutely fine. Along the way, we would at the very least learn a lot of new things and gain better arguments.

> *Your first impulse should always be to find the evidence that disconfirms your most cherished beliefs and those of others. That is true science.*
> – Robert Greene

I understand that finding a way through the mayhem of information is a lot of work and it is tempting to simply follow expert opinions and authority. Some truths, however, are not simply brought to you, not even by common experts. You will have to go and find them yourself. If experts find new evidence about a topic but the facts are not politically correct, they would not be openly discussed. You might never even hear about such truths, because people around you are afraid to share them or do also not know about them in the first place. So you must dig even further to find them. And what is true is sometimes harder to find than what is not wrong. Because all too often people place what they like to believe or what fits in above reality.

If you actually saw an alien yourself, likely, no one would believe you. Not even if you had evidence and you had it on camera. Except, of course, for those who love mysterious things. They will believe you, even without evidence. Most people, however, would always find a way to dismiss your evidence. Until the mainstream media reports about it and it becomes the mainstream narrative. If you had 100% proof for something, what does the evidence matter to the world if no one is willing to take a look at it? Even if all the evidence was just one step around the corner, most people would not be willing to take that step around the corner. They would rather listen to the stories they have been told about what is around the corner, without having a look themselves. But, oftentimes, the information is right there and we just need people who are willing to take that small step and go to see themselves. People that are skeptical yet interested. If you want to find the information that no one is interested in bringing to you, then you will have to actively look for it. There are plenty of truths we will never find if we do not actively go and have a look.

Another important skill we need, to find truth, is to be able to re-evaluate our own views and beliefs. Not every second of every day, but sporadically, with an objective view and the sincere will to improve our perspective. Maybe you were very convinced but missed a piece of the puzzle. Maybe there was a bias in you that you overlooked. Maybe you got tricked into a simple thought that turned out to be more complex. Maybe you believed one thing but when you hear another perspective, it changes your mind. When you hear one narrative, it may seem so logical, and everything makes sense. When you hear the arguments of another narrative, everything there might make even more sense and all other arguments seem weak. Many things in life are complex and difficult to understand and most often, there are valid arguments in various directions. But being wrong at times is not a sign of not using Root Access Life. Root Access Life comprises of accepting our own errors and tendencies, and being willing to correct them as soon as we know better. There are moments when predictions turn out to be completely mistaken. When conclusions that seemed so obvious turn out to be false. We should embrace such moments. They are beautiful in that they teach us to be humble and open-minded.

> *Be willing to see the objective truth, whatever it might be.*
>
> *Ask yourself how would you behave if you found strong evidence supporting something that goes against your current belief. Would you be open to the possibility that this might be true? You might not be easily convinced, but are you open to the possibility?*
>
> *This openness is highly important in order to come closer to what is true.*

Conspiracy Fanatics vs Mainstream Propaganda Fanatics

Political correctness is tyranny with manners.
– Charlton Heston

Are you flexible, as a queen, to think objectively about touchy subjects? Are you influenced by society to get triggered by the word "conspiracy"? Whenever there is a hypersensitive topic in a society, like "conspiracy theories", it is probably a good idea to quietly take a step back and think objectively about it. A conspiracy is basically a secret plan of two or more people, intended to reach personal goals that are not necessarily in the interest of outsiders. Perhaps to gain power, manipulate and control others. Such conspiracies exist in this world in countless numbers, whether we like it or not. Heck, we have technically probably even been conspirers ourselves. At some point in childhood, we told our friends not to tell our mom about something bad we did at school. That would technically be a conspiracy. The conspiracy theory is obviously the theory about a conspiracy. If our mother then guessed that we are hiding something from her and our friends were silent about it too, she was technically a "conspiracy theorist". Of course, when we talk about the word "conspiracy theory", we think about governments, large companies and organizations or powerful individuals having secret plans. Although we never know their exact plans, it is not unthinkable and even quite obvious that governments, companies, organizations or rich individuals hold back information on some level, favoring their own interests. It can often be proven retrospectively and it is not that crazy to at least assume so, in many instances. When a new president steps into office, he or she will be confronted with a lot of secret, inside information. Some of this secret information may be in favor of the own nation or perhaps even of only the government itself, while being less in the wishes of other nations or the public. This is, by definition, a conspiracy and it is nothing extraordinary at all. As long as humans exist, conspiracies will exist.

Some people never believe any conspiracy theory because of the bad reputation of that word: "conspiracy theorist". Others always believe every conspiracy theory they get to hear. Only a few will be able to think objectively about every new topic and every new situation that arises, to see truths and faults in theories and to question the subject matter in all aspects.

Are you able to talk and think about possible conspiracies with an open mind? Are you too quickly believing conspiracy theories or are you perhaps too quickly discarding them?

If you are able to examine them critically and come up with pros and cons about any specific theory, congratulations! You are most certainly being a queen and you are most certainly making use of Root Access Life!

Do you believe that the pharmaceutical industry only wants you to be as healthy as possible? That corrupt governments and companies only exist in faraway countries? That people who are driven by greed for money, power and control only existed a long time ago or in movies? That the mass media always tells you the full truth? Or do you perhaps believe that the whole world is only about money and power. That everybody just lies to control you and every doctor only sells you fear and poison to keep you sick?

Some people tend to be extremely naive about this world and about the motives of humans. Others excessively focus on the dark sides of humanity, leaders and systems. There is a tendency that people either blindly trust everything that authorities say, or that they distrust everything and come up with conspiracy theories over absolutely everything. To be fair, there are endless crazy theories in this world. It is, therefore, understandable that people like to trust the official version of a story. Admittedly, on the other hand, a lot of untrustworthy things have happened in this world. It's, therefore, easy to have doubt towards the mainstream media and to come up with conspiracy theories. Both tendencies are comprehensible. But as you already know, Root Access Life implies being able to see things from more than just one fixated angle. Of course, there are plenty of actual conspiracies in this world, but we have to admit that we are not psychics and we can't read people's minds. We can theorize but we should stay on the ground and admit that not everything is a conspiracy. At the same time, we should not be so naive to think that we are not being manipulated in many areas and in many ways.

> *Do not blindly trust anything, but also do not blindly dismiss anything.*
> – Unknown

As we know, most people tend to go to one extreme or the other. This is especially true on the spectrum of controversial topics. In this case, on one side there are the so-called "conspiracy theorists" and on the other side are the radical politically correct.

It doesn't make sense, though, to call conspiracy theorists "extreme". It's the "conspiracy fanatic" that can become rather extreme. A theory is a theory and everyone should theorize as much as he or she wants. Every good invention came through theories and from people who were particularly good at theorizing. Every detective theorizes to find a criminal. Every time a mystery was solved, a corrupt system was exposed or a study was conducted, it was due to initial theorizing. The ability to theorize is great, yet, of course, we don't want to over-theorize things. Theories become a problem when we get too convinced and almost obsessed over them. When we forget what they are: simply theories. This can create what I call "conspiracy fanaticism".

Seeing things from a more politically correct angle, on the other hand, is not extreme either. It is the "mainstream propaganda fanaticism" that can become rather extreme and problematic.

"Mainstream propaganda fanatics" largely ignore how severely greed for money, power and control dominates their own country and the systems they use and live in. They follow the hype, official-sounding information and whatever the mainstream news within their political system tells them, disregarding the fact that conspiracies have and always will exist. We just can't always see them easily. But that is what conspiracies are intended for; not letting people see through them too easily. There might be far more false theories than there are actual conspiracies, but many conspiracies exist, nonetheless.

It is interesting to observe, how "mainstream propaganda fanatics" can also have conspiracy theories. They just won't have them against official entities or governments, but against unofficial or unpopular entities and against any unofficial source. "Mainstream propaganda fanatics" deeply and naively believe that all important information will come to them via the mainstream media or the mainstream narrative. They deeply believe that if there was evidence or good information, the mainstream would have adopted the belief already and every official mainstream news channel would already talk about it.

The majority of the people focus on the news of the current day, they get heated by it and then they move on to the news of the next day. None of them would even notice if a conspiracy theory actually became true after all. Similarly, a "conspiracy fanatic" jumps from believing one theory to the next, convinced of the new conspiracy story of the day from an "unofficial" news channel. They would not even look back and see how many conspiracy theories turned out to be false.

Even if a conspiracy theory was true, there will always be crazy people believing even those theories that are untrue. That should not keep you from thinking for yourself and informing yourself about it. Likewise, there will always be naive people supporting anything that is on the mainstream news. That does not mean that it is always wrong. And it should not keep you from also questioning all the "underground" news channels and every single conspiracy theory.

Do you see how "mainstream propaganda fanatics" and the "conspiracy fanatics" actually have a lot in common? Both are fanatic, both are not open-minded and both are not queens. "Conspiracy fanatics" like mysteries more, while the "mainstream propaganda fanatics" mostly love things officially explained, in order and confirmed by mainstream authority. The "mainstream propaganda fanatics" are too easily persuaded by buzzwords like "official information", "scientific", "new study" or "expert opinion". The "conspiracy fanatics" are too easily persuaded by words like "manipulation", "secret plan", "elites", "new world order", "corruption". Both parties can be rather gullible and often don't check their information very carefully. They are not open to the fact that something may be true that does not correspond to their world view. The "mainstream propaganda fanatics" are immediately ready to call everything a conspiracy theory. They are gullible towards anything that sounds official and is represented by the masses. If someone has the "conspiracy theorist" stamp, they will despise that person no matter what that person actually says. This is not much different to "conspiracy fanatics", who are less fanatic about the mainstream news, but about any information that feeds them more theories.

Do you realize that there is a saner approach? We can accept that there are conspiracies in this world and we can try our best to see through them while staying on the ground with our theories. I personally like to theorize and I find it interesting to try and understand possible secret plans, corruption and abuse of power. There is absolutely nothing wrong with theorizing that way. As long as one does not get too convinced without having good evidence. And as long as one does not get obsessed with a theory. Just as much, as it is not wrong to watch the mainstream news and absorb bits of information from it, while subsequently researching more independently on the subject matter. As long as one does not get too convinced without thinking autonomously. And as long as one does not get obsessed with the mainstream narrative.

Since we don't have a crystal ball to know everything or to read people's minds, we have to stay grounded. We cannot see all motives of people and secret plans and systems. Therefore, being convinced that nobody has a secret plan is just as much of a theory as saying there is a plan behind it. We could also say one is the "conspiracy theory" and the other is the "anti-conspiracy theory", while both are just theories. Because believing that a conspiracy is not true is, in a way, also a theory. Unless you yourself are, or were, involved behind the scenes, of course.

If you want to be skeptical towards conspiracy theories and debunk them, by all means do so. Make sure, however, to do the research yourself and to encounter all sides of the evidence. Not just on the mainstream narrative or the opinions of your friends.

Be open that some of those theories are less crazy as they appear at first. When we have access to our root and there is good enough evidence, we might theorize over a conspiracy. If there is good enough evidence, we might believe the mainstream narrative. We might even be drawn towards one side more than to the other. But, in any case, we can once again ask ourselves if we sincerely want to know the truth and are sincerely interested in reality.

The fact that something is labeled as a "conspiracy theory" should not have any influence on what you believe. Anyone can call anything whatever they want. What counts is the actual available evidence and your autonomous thinking. If you fully trust a theory solely based on the word "corruption", your settings may be grayed out. Or if you disregard information solely based on the word "conspiracy theory", your settings may be grayed out. Beneath all programming and settings, you can think about anything, and you can look objectively at any information in the world yourself.

Never Lie to Yourself

Above all, don't lie to yourself. The man who lies to himself and listens to his own lie comes to a point that he cannot distinguish the truth within him, or around him, and so loses all respect for himself and for others. And having no respect he ceases to love.
– Fyodor Dostoevsky

One amazing human quality is for us to be very adaptive to our environment, to the people surrounding us and the circumstances we are facing. Adjusting to situations and changing the way we talk and act, depending on who we are interacting with, is a useful ability to have. While it is important and useful to be socially aware and calibrated, it raises the question of whether we are true to ourselves or not. "Just be yourself" is one common advice we are taught. But who am I? Am I a specific persona or character?

If I have an important job interview, I certainly want to present myself in a specific way to have a chance of getting the job. Other parts of me might not be well seen in a job interview, yet they are a part of me, nonetheless. So, am I the person that is well seen at the job interview, or the one that is not well seen? Am I both at the same time, or are both just a reflection of my social environment?

We may take the advice to just be ourselves as an encouragement to find a specific personality, a specific style, behavior and a specific way to talk, act and think. But With Root Access Life we are versatile, like a queen and we are not one programmed idea of a person. We are free to act however we want, free to change the things we do, the interests we follow and the people we meet. We are free to change the way we think, behave and what we focus on. Just as Root Access Life gives us the ability to view things from different angles and to change the way we look at things, it also gives us the ability to change the way we act or the mindset we adopt. So, the answer to the question "who am I?" should be: whoever I want to be in this moment. Of course, always accompanied by my unique experiences, knowledge, talents, preferences and characteristics. But we do not have to fit into any strict category.

The roles we play in this life are all, in a way, a part of us, while at the same time not being attached to us at all. Society wants us to be that persona, predictable and put in a box, because it is very convenient for society if everyone has their own tag and if everything is categorized. In reality, we are much more than that tag or the box we put each other in.

We are more than just one specific character; we are adaptable and we can change our focus and behaviors. We can dress up very noble and still be down to earth and friendly. We can dress cool and have a warm heart at the same time. We can look well behaved, but completely act out. We don't have to be programmed like robots to be only a certain way.

But am I lying if I play different roles and characters? We can all, at times, find it hard to be completely honest with others and we might sometimes hide our thoughts and emotions in an effort to protect ourselves.

Using Root Access Life does not mean having pure, innocent and perfect thoughts, emotions and impulses at all times. Or that we always share everything with the outside world. But using Root Access Life can manifest in acknowledging our inner processes and admitting them to ourselves. It can manifest in being aware and reflecting ourselves objectively and with kindness. Others may lie to us and there may have been times when we have lied to others. In any case and above all, we should never lie to ourselves. When we do not lie to ourselves, we become, in a way, authentic, regardless of how we adapt in the outside world. Whatever role we are in and however we decide to behave, it is wise to never lie to ourselves about our thoughts, emotions, behaviors desires and motives. We can adapt the way we talk, what words, body language and what tone of voice we use, while acknowledging our adaptive behavior. When we lie to ourselves, we live miserably. But when we build a truthful and friendly connection with ourselves, we can choose freely to be whoever we want. And to change our behavior, with awareness and authenticity.

Perhaps you have some feelings or thoughts that you would not be too proud of sharing, or that would not be well accepted by others. At least you are capable of sharing your thoughts and emotions with yourself. We can admit to ourselves, for example, that we are jealous sometimes and we can accept it as a natural human emotion. The very fact that we get more aware of such reactions makes the difference. What makes us authentic is not to fixate over one role. It is the ability to observe ourselves and accept our ever-changing thoughts, emotions and impulses.

Being truthful to ourselves, we can be our own good friend. If our best friend has a problem, we tend to give the best, most honest and straightforward advice. We are clear and honest, but warm, motivating and supportive. Our self-talk can become the same. So, the next time you make a mistake or have unpleasant thoughts, emotions or biases, you can admit them to yourself, knowing there will only be understanding and support, without judgement.

Be honest with yourself and never lie to yourself about your motives, thoughts, emotions and behaviors. Acknowledge them with kindness and understanding.

A Piece of Clay

All that happens to us, including our humiliations, our misfortunes, our embarrassments, all is given to us as raw material, as clay, so that we may shape our art.
– Jorge Luis Borges

The word prejudgment literally refers to a judgment in advance of knowing. A judgment is not changeable and neither is a prejudgment. Having prejudgments is not a good idea, because it leads to premature and fixated conclusions. There is, on the other hand, nothing wrong with having preconceptions. In fact, it is absolutely normal. We may want to try to reduce our preconceptions at times or become more aware of them, but they never completely stop. Our brain naturally evaluates people and environments. This is important, because it helps us to assess and predict situations and to possibly protect ourselves. The essential part is that we are able to change those preconceptions if necessary. When we have a preconception about something or someone and we are able to change it, we can't call it prejudgment. If we use Root Access Life, it doesn't mean we never have preconceptions, but that we never have prejudgments. Because we are always able to adjust our preconceptions if necessary. Just as the queen can always change her direction on the chessboard, you can always make changes to anything you assumed. In many cases, our preconceptions, our gut feeling, our intuition, our experiences, turn out to be right. However, if at any point our preconceptions turn out to be false or inadequate, we can simply make changes to them. Everyone has the ability to make such changes, however big or small they might be. Misconceptions are a part of life and they are part of our learning process.

Let's imagine every single person, every situation and every topic we come across as a piece of modeling clay. Everything and everyone we experience starts off with the exact same shape. As soon as we have a preconception in our mind, we form a figure out of the clay. When we get to know anything about a person, topic or situation, we start remodeling the clay. Our perception of a person, situation or topic will change again and again. The beautiful thing is that, at any point in time, we can slightly reshape that piece of clay. And if we have a misconception about someone or something, we simply remodel it. However that clay may look throughout time, we can accept it as it is right now, and that we might have to make small changes in the future. While the structure gives us strong indications, it is not a fixated mass that cannot be changed.

A lot of things in this world might be similar but they come in different versions, shapes and forms. While we might form different shapes and figures out of our clay, we can accept it as it is. There is no point in striving to make every sculpture in our mind look the same. In a politically correct society, we may be pushed into the idea that in order to have equality, everything has to be exactly the same. The idea is that everybody is the same and, therefore, we should respect everybody. This, however, reinforces the idea that whatever is different should not be respected. The world is a complex organism with vast variousness and it houses different humans, animals, plants and materials. If we need everything to be the same in order to respect it, we would disrespect a lot of things and living beings on this planet. Having equality does not require everything to be equal, but to accept and even honor what is different.

This also applies to using Root Access Life. Talking down on people who seemingly do not use it yet would be like a teacher laughing at students for not knowing all the answers before the class. One teacher is specialized in a subject, but the same teacher can be taught by someone else in another field. After reading this book, you may be specialized in Root Access Life, while seeking assistance in another area.

Everybody's life is a story and by asking and listening, we get to hear the most interesting tales. No matter how programmed a person seems to us, be genuinely interested in that person and a surprise is almost guaranteed. It does not matter if we disagree with a person in some areas. Everyone has a unique, interesting life story to share and, when we listen carefully and ask questions, we might suddenly understand that person's point of view. Almost guaranteed, our modeling clay will look much different if we actually start to listen and show interest in a person. Through listening and through genuine interest in people, animals and all things in the world, we will start seeing a lot of remodeling that is required. The remodeling of the sculpture that represents our perception of the world.

Whenever you make a prediction or presumptions, imagine a figure of clay that can be adjusted accordingly when further information is available.

Conclusion

It takes incredible interest, openness and willingness to read through a book like this and to confront ourselves with such complex and mind-twisting topics. Most certainly, it requires Root Access Life. As life is not a game of chess and chess rules do not apply in the real world, there are not only two hostile queens. Instead, we can all be amicable queens and live among each other, being versatile and flexible. May this book inspire you to ask new questions, to take new perspectives and to continue living with Root Access Life. The quest for knowledge and understanding is never-ending, but through the pursuit of unprogrammed thinking, our mind is free.

Joah Ralf

For more information about the author and his work visit: rootaccesslife.com